Reforming Nuclear Export Controls

The Future of the Nuclear Suppliers Group

W0114158

sipri

Stockholm International Peace Research Institute
Signalistgatan 9, SE-169 70 Solna, Sweden
Telephone: 46 8/655 97 00
Fax: 46 8/655 97 33
Email: sipri@sipri.org
URL: http://www.sipri.org

Reforming Nuclear Export Controls

The Future of the Nuclear Suppliers Group

SIPRI Research Report No. 22

**Ian Anthony, Christer Ahlström
and Vitaly Fedchenko**

OXFORD UNIVERSITY PRESS
2007

This book has been printed digitally and produced in a standard specification
in order to ensure its continuing availability

OXFORD
UNIVERSITY PRESS

Great Clarendon Street, Oxford OX2 6DP
United Kingdom

Oxford University Press is a department of the University of Oxford.
It furthers the University's objective of excellence in research, scholarship,
and education by publishing worldwide. Oxford is a registered trade mark of
Oxford University Press in the UK and in certain other countries

© SIPRI 2007

First published 2007
Reprinted 2012

British Library Cataloguing in Publication Data
Data available

Library of Congress Cataloging in Publication Data
Data available

This book is also available in electronic format at
http://books.sipri.org/

ISBN 978-0-19-929086-4

Contents

Preface

Since the years 2001–2002 when the risk of nuclear weapon proliferation was propelled afresh to the top of the international security agenda, much debate and effort—sometimes with serious security consequences of its own—has been focused on the threat from individual 'problem states'. The real extent of the challenge, however, only becomes clear when what might be called the world's nuclear economy is contemplated as a whole. The problem starts with the fact that the key technologies used today for nuclear energy production are all inherently capable of being hijacked for weapons development. It continues with the fact that these technologies are now more widely dispersed around the world than ever, and that an even wider range of countries are forecast to increase their reliance on nuclear energy in future. The Non-Proliferation Treaty (NPT) establishes the right norms and principles to stop this legitimate use from spawning new weapons programmes, but more than one country recently has worked under cover of NPT provisions to build up the expertise needed for a break-out to weapons capability. On top of all this, the traditional treaty system is ill-adapted to catch proliferation-related activities by non-state actors ranging from scientists to terrorists.

This Research Report, compiled by two SIPRI nuclear experts and a former SIPRI Deputy Director, takes the challenges facing the Nuclear Suppliers Group (NSG) as a starting point to explore a cluster of linked practical, legal, and political issues. The NSG is a group of states traditionally strong in nuclear technology that cooperate to stop risky and irresponsible international transfers of related materials and knowledge. The group's credibility and effectiveness is constantly under test from the general demand to update and refine its techniques, from the need to bond more effectively with other institutions and processes working in the same field, and from contradictions that arise in the handling of individual cases (those of Iran and India are singled out in this volume). Hanging over the NSG and its members is the larger issue of whether it is any longer fair, or efficient, to reserve the control of a wide range of nuclear transactions to a self-appointed group with a limited, traditional composition. This Report ends by discussing how the work of control might be shared in a more inclusive way, both with the whole community of responsible states, and with other concerned actors such as the private business sector.

In the present state of the non-proliferation debate, it is SIPRI's hope that this fact-rich and balanced analysis may be helpful to readers both within and beyond the expert nuclear circle. I am grateful to Ian Anthony, Christer Ahlström and Vitaly Fedchenko for putting together the pieces of this Research Report, and to Tom Gill for the editing.

Alyson J. K. Bailes
Director, SIPRI
August 2007

Abbreviations and acronyms

ABACC	Brazilian–Argentine Agency for Accounting and Control of Nuclear Materials
AEA	1954 Atomic Energy Act
AEOI	Atomic Energy Organization of Iran
CEFIC	European Chemical Industry Council
CGEA	Community General Export Authorization
CEO	Chief executive officer
CIA	US Central Intelligence Agency
CIS	Commonwealth of Independent States
CITS	Center for International Trade and Security
CNCI	US–Indian Civil Nuclear Cooperation Initiative
COCOM	Coordinating Committee for Multilateral Export Controls
CTBT	Comprehensive Nuclear Test Ban Treaty
DAE	Department of Atomic Energy (India)
EDP	Equipment or material especially designed or prepared for the processing, use or production of special fissionable material
EU	European Union
Euratom	European Atomic Energy Community
GE	General Electric (USA)
G8	Group of Eight industrialized nations
HEU	Highly enriched uranium
IAEA	International Atomic Energy Agency
ITER	International Thermonuclear Experimental Reactor
JIE	Joint Information Exchange
LEU	Low-enriched uranium
Minatom	Ministry of Atomic Energy (Russia)
MOX	Mixed oxide
MOU	Memorandum of understanding
MTCR	Missile Technology Control Regime

NAM	Non-Aligned Movement
NBC	Nuclear, biological and chemical (weapons)
NNPA	1978 Nuclear Non-Proliferation Act
NPCIL	Nuclear Power Corporation of India Limted
NPT	Treaty on the Non-Proliferation of Nuclear Weapons
NSG	Nuclear Suppliers Group
NSSP	Next Steps in Strategic Partnership
OECD	Organisation for Economic Co-operation and Development
OEG	Operational Expert Group
POST	Parliamentary Office of Science and Technology
PSI	Proliferation Security Initiative
SAFE	2005 Framework of Standards to Secure and Facilitate Global Trade
SCCC	The Common System for Accounting and Control of Nuclear Materials [Sistema Común de Contabilidad y Control de Materiales Nucleares]
UN	United Nations
UNMOVIC	UN Monitoring, Verification and Inspection Commission
WMD	Weapons of mass destruction

1. Introduction

At present, few countries possess all the elements of a full nuclear fuel cycle, and the great majority rely on foreign sources for at least some items that are critical for the development of a civilian or military nuclear programme. The existence of a nuclear power industry and of other peaceful uses of nuclear technology requires international transactions that involve the materials, equipment and technologies that could make a technical contribution to a nuclear weapon capability. This Research Report surveys and discusses current efforts to develop and implement export controls for items used in the development of nuclear weapons.

Preventing the acquisition of nuclear weapons by states that do not already possess them is currently one of the central policy objectives of the international community. The need to fashion a more effective set of measures to achieve this objective has taken on a new urgency in conditions where senior officials, such as Mohamed ElBaradei, the Director General of the International Atomic Energy Agency (IAEA), anticipate a growing risk that proliferation-relevant technologies will continue to be spread more widely. ElBaradei has stated that, whereas equipment, material and training were once largely inaccessible, 'Today . . . there is a sophisticated worldwide network that can deliver systems for producing material usable in [nuclear] weapons. The demand clearly exists: countries remain interested in the illicit acquisition of weapons of mass destruction.'[1]

The example of North Korea has highlighted the risk that countries can engage in proliferation-sensitive activities such as fuel making and fuel reprocessing, transparently and under safeguards, but then apply these same techniques for military purposes. In 2003 North Korea was the first state to withdraw from the 1968 Treaty on the Non-Proliferation of Nuclear Weapons (Non-Proliferation Treaty, NPT).[2] Using a reactor acquired ostensibly for peaceful research,

---

[1] ElBaradei, M., 'Saving ourselves from destruction', *New York Times*, 12 Feb. 2004.

[2] See the text of the NPT on the UN disarmament website, <http://disarmament.un.org/TreatyStatus.nsf>.

North Korea extracted plutonium from spent reactor fuel and, according to its own statements, used it to make nuclear weapons.[3] Analysts have drawn attention to the risk that additional breakouts from the NPT might further destabilize the regional and global security environment.[4] However, because the military and civilian uses of nuclear technology are inextricably linked, the risk of breakout is embedded in the structure of the current global nuclear industry. The IAEA observes the machinery of production and accounts for nuclear material in those parts of the nuclear complex that states party to the NPT declare to the IAEA, but this may not be enough to determine whether facilities are intended purely for civil use or for potential weaponization.[5]

If uncertainties about the use to which nuclear technologies are being put become widespread, other states could choose to follow a 'hedge' strategy by carrying out research on industrial techniques for producing the types of fissile material used in nuclear weapons. These states may prefer to have the option of producing a nuclear weapon at fairly short notice and without being dependent on foreign sources of material or technology. In support of that option these countries may build facilities and infrastructure that would give them the technical capacity to initiate a nuclear weapon programme if a political decision were taken to do so.

To reduce such potential uncertainties, states have recognized that it is necessary to strengthen national and international nuclear non-proliferation mechanisms. Several recent proposals have been put forward by governments and by the IAEA in an effort to reduce the risk that legitimate international commerce in nuclear and nuclear-related dual-use items might contribute to nuclear weapon proliferation.

Concerns about nuclear proliferation are being addressed against the background of a renewed interest in the potential contribution that nuclear power could make to global energy supply. ElBaradei has stated that 'the more we look to the future, the more we can expect

[3] Korean Central News Agency, 'DPRK FM on its stand to suspend its participation in six-party talks for indefinite period', 10 Feb. 2005, <http://www.kcna.co.jp/item/2005/200502/news02/11.htm#1>.

[4] Ekéus, R., 'Challenges to the international non-proliferation regime', Paper presented at the First Anniversary Proliferation Security Initiative Meeting, Krakow, 31 May–1 June 2004, <http://www.msz.gov.pl/docs/172/PSI_CRAKOW.pdf>.

[5] For an outline of IAEA nuclear accounting procedures see IAEA, *IAEA Safeguards Glossary: 2001 Edition*, International Nuclear Verification Series no. 3 (2001), <http://www-pub.iaea.org/MTCD/publications/PDF/nvs-3-cd/PDF/NVS3_prn.pdf>, pp. 45–57.

countries to be considering the potential benefits that expanding nuclear power has to offer for the global environment and for economic growth'.[6] This greater interest would translate into a significant increase in the volume of international trade in nuclear and nuclear-related materials, equipment and technologies.

While international transactions are legal and necessary, responsible governments control international transfers of nuclear and dual-use items by making certain that an assessment of each transaction takes place before the items concerned leave the jurisdiction of the regulating authority. International cooperation can help governments establish and enforce effective controls, although this cooperation does not substitute for their legal responsibilities.

Efforts to align criteria governing nuclear exports can be traced to the 1950s.[7] The Nuclear Suppliers Group (NSG) was established in 1978 following three years of discussion among seven nuclear supplier countries—Canada, France, the Federal Republic of Germany, Japan, the Soviet Union, the United Kingdom and the United States. It is an informal group of nuclear supplier states that seeks to prevent the acquisition of nuclear weapons by countries other than those recognized as nuclear weapon states in the framework of the NPT—China, France, Russia, the UK and the USA. As of January 2007 the NSG had 45 participating states (see table 2.1, chapter 2).

The NSG has developed standards that participating states apply when making national decisions about what exports to authorize. These are the Guidelines for Nuclear Transfers and Guidelines for Nuclear-Related Dual-Use Equipment, Materials, Software and Related Technology. It has also drawn up lists of items to which these guidelines apply. The IAEA publishes these guidelines and lists in its Information Circular INFCIRC/254.[8]

INFCIRC/254 lists items that should not be exported without prior assessment and authorization by responsible national authorities in

[6] IAEA, 'Nuclear power's changing future', Press release 2004/05, 26 June 2004, <http://www.iaea.org/NewsCenter/PressReleases/2004/prn200405.html>.

[7] van Dassen, L., 'Sweden', ed. H. Müller, *Nuclear Export Controls in Europe* (European Interuniversity Press: Brussels, 1995), p. 187.

[8] The guidelines on nuclear exports are contained in part I of INFCIRC/254, and those on dual-use exports are in part II of INFCIRC/254. The most recent version of part I of the NSG Guidelines is INFCIRC/254/Rev.6/Part 1, 16 May 2003. The most recent version of part II of the NSG Guidelines is INFCIRC/254/Rev.5/Part 2, 16 May 2003. Both sets of guidelines, as well as most other INFCIRCs and IAEA documents, are available from the IAEA website at <http://www.iaea.org/Publications/Documents/index.html>.

NSG participating states. These lists represent an informal agreement about what needs to be subject to control. They do not have any legal authority until they are incorporated into legislation that is binding on exporters in the participating states. In most cases this will be national laws but in the case of the European Union (EU) the primary legislation that controls many of the items listed in INFCIRC/254 has been made part of EU law through EU Council Regulation 1334/2000.[9] This regulation established a common EU export control system for dual-use items, including an annex containing a list of the items subject to control.

There is a legitimate international market for nuclear technologies and the NPT contains provisions, in Article IV, that underline 'the inalienable right of all the Parties to the Treaty to develop research, production and use of nuclear energy for peaceful purposes without discrimination and in conformity with Articles I and II of this Treaty'. Article IV refers to the right of all parties to facilitate and 'to participate in, the fullest possible exchange of equipment, materials and scientific and technological information for the peaceful uses of nuclear energy'.

The extent to which this commitment has been honoured in the past is questioned by analysts who believe that countries that own advanced nuclear technologies see them as commercial assets, which they cannot be forced to share with those whom they disapprove of or who cannot pay the price. It has been asserted that the development of nuclear export controls is evidence that nuclear suppliers have progressively moved away from the 'grand bargain' underpinning the NPT—that states would forgo nuclear weapons in exchange for active disarmament by existing nuclear weapon states as well as a commitment by those states to facilitate international nuclear cooperation for peaceful purposes.[10] Writing about the need for export control reform,

---

[9] The regulation is normally amended on an annual basis to take into account changes in the control list that forms an integral part of the law. The most recent version at the time of writing is 'Council Regulation (EC) no. 394/2006 of 27 February 2006 amending and updating Regulation (EC) no. 1334/2000 setting up a Community regime for the control of exports of dual-use items and technology', *Official Journal of the European Union*, L73 (13 Mar. 2006).

[10] 'Many in the developing world, however, feel that the grand bargain enshrined in the NPT has been forgotten by the world's major powers, while multilateral export controls are viewed as a growing impediment to international technology transfers that are essential to their economic development.' Henry L. Stimson Center and Stanley Foundation, 'Event summary: improving multilateral export controls and technology access for the developing

an Indian scholar has asserted that 'maintaining technological superiority over other nations, including friendly nations, continues to be an important aspect of safeguarding national security for most sovereign nations'.[11]

These assertions are rejected by the NSG participating states, which have expressed the view that the activities of the group actually help to promote the objectives of the NPT. According to this view, the guidelines facilitate legitimate nuclear trade by providing a mechanism that permits nuclear cooperation in a manner consistent with international nuclear non-proliferation norms.[12] If the governments of exporting states were to regard the risk of proliferation as too high, they would prohibit, rather than seek to control, exports. The alternative to effective export controls would be less, rather than more, international nuclear cooperation.

The discovery of the worldwide illicit nuclear trafficking network of Pakistani scientist Abdul Qadeer Khan has led to a greater focus on improving regulation of international nuclear cooperation.[13] Statements and initiatives by the USA, among other states, as well as by the EU and the Group of Eight (G8) industrialized nations have paid closer attention to the actual and potential role of the NSG in such regulation.

In February 2004 US President George W. Bush called on the NSG participating states to refuse to sell uranium enrichment and reprocessing technologies to any state that does not already possess full-scale, functioning enrichment or spent-fuel reprocessing plants.[14] In

world', Washington, DC, Dec. 2002 <http://www.stimson.org/exportcontrol/events.cfm?ID=46>, p. 2,

[11] Mallik, A., *Technology and Security in the 21st Century: A Demand-side Perspective*, SIPRI Research Report no. 20 (Oxford University Press: Oxford, 2004), p. 124.

[12] IAEA, 'The Nuclear Suppliers Group: its origins, role and activities', Attachment to communication of 28 August 2003 received from the Government of the United States of America on behalf of the member states of the Nuclear Suppliers Group, INFCIRC/539/Rev.2, 16 Sep. 2003.

[13] Beginning in the mid-1970s, Khan developed a covert international procurement network to support Pakistan's nuclear weapon programme. During the 1990s this network was used to facilitate the clandestine procurement of items for the nuclear programmes of other countries, including Iran and Libya. For a description see Kile, S. N., 'Nuclear arms control and non-proliferation', *SIPRI Yearbook 2005: Armaments, Disarmament and International Security* (Oxford University Press: Oxford, 2005), pp. 552–55.

[14] The White House, Office of the Press Secretary, 'President announces new measures to counter the threat of WMD', Fort Lesley J. McNair, National Defense University, Washington, DC, 11 Feb. 2004, <http://www.whitehouse.gov/news/releases/2004/02/20040211-4.html>.

the same speech he also proposed that only states that have signed an Additional Protocol to their safeguards agreement with the IAEA should be allowed to import equipment for their civilian nuclear programmes.[15]

As part of the Action Plan on Nonproliferation agreed at their 2004 summit meeting, the G8 agreed to 'work to amend appropriately the NSG Guidelines, and to gain the widest possible support for such measures in the future'.[16] In line with this objective, the G8 leaders agreed on a one-year moratorium on any new initiatives involving transferring enrichment and reprocessing technologies to states that did not already possess them and called on other states to adopt the same approach.

The EU member states are also working within the NSG towards making the adoption of the Additional Protocol a condition of supply for nuclear exports. Moreover, the EU has supported amending the NSG Guidelines to require an immediate suspension of the supply of nuclear materials, equipment and technology to those in breach of their safeguards obligations.[17]

Given what is known about the history of nuclear weapon programmes, the very significant role that export controls have recently been given in non-proliferation strategies was arguably an overdue development. The North Korean case noted above was not the first time that countries have made use of facilities and items of equipment and technology ostensibly acquired for peaceful purposes in weapon programmes. The nuclear weapon capabilities of India, Israel and Pakistan depended heavily on imported technologies. The creation of the NSG was a response to India's decision to divert plutonium that had been produced in a reactor provided by Canada for peaceful nuclear research for use in a nuclear explosive device in 1974.[18]

---

[15] For a description of IAEA safeguards and the Additional Protocol see chapter 2 in this volume, section IV.

[16] G8, 'Sea Island Summit 2004: G8 Action Plan on Nonproliferation', Sea Island, Ga., 9 June 2004, <http://www.g8.utoronto.ca/summit/2004seaisland/nonproliferation.html>.

[17] Statement at the Main Committee II of the 2005 Review Conference of the Parties to the Treaty on the Non-Proliferation of Nuclear Weapons by Mr. Paul Kayser, Ambassador, on behalf of the European Union, New York, N.Y. 19 May 2005, <http://europa-eu-un.org/articles/en/article_4719_en.htm>.

[18] Timerbaev, R., *Gruppa Yadernykh Postavshchikov: Istoriya Sozdaniya (1974–1978)* [The Nuclear Suppliers Group: why and how it was created (1974–1978)] (PIR Center: Moscow, 2000), p. 21.

India, Israel and Pakistan have not signed the NPT. Moreover, India and Israel acquired the facilities, equipment and technology that played a key role in military programmes before July 1968, when the NPT was opened for signature.[19] However, recent cases of great concern from a nuclear proliferation standpoint have involved states that were parties to the NPT at the time they acquired equipment and technology under what has been described as a 'misrepresentation' of civilian use.[20]

There have now been three confirmed cases (Iraq, North Korea and Libya) of states acquiring nuclear technology with the intention of developing nuclear weapons at a time when they were parties to the NPT. In another case that has raised significant international concern, Iran has designed and is constructing a facility that will be able to carry out uranium enrichment on an industrial scale. In 2003 it was also confirmed that Iran was building a very large facility to produce heavy water—used in some nuclear reactors capable of producing weapon-grade plutonium. These projects have attracted attention and suspicion because they were carried out in a clandestine manner. The existence of these particular nuclear activities in Iran, Iraq and North Korea became public against the wishes of the respective governments and in each case further details have only been disclosed after concerted international pressure.

I. The dual-use nature of nuclear technology

The risk that states will exploit international cooperation to develop military capacities is inherent in the nature of current nuclear technologies. All known types of the nuclear fuel cycle utilize fission of so-called fissile isotopes: uranium-235 (U-235), plutonium-239 (Pu-239) or U-233.[21] These isotopes also happen to be those most suit-

---

[19] Although the NPT did not then exist, bilateral agreements on the peaceful use of nuclear items were in place with supplier countries before sensitive technologies were transferred. The use of imported technologies in military programmes violated these bilateral agreements.

[20] Reiss, M. B., 'The nuclear tipping point: prospects for a world of many nuclear weapons states', eds K. M. Campbell, R. J. Einhorn and M. B. Reiss, *The Nuclear Tipping Point: Why States Reconsider Their Nuclear Choices* (Brookings Institution: Washington, DC, 2004), p. 8.

[21] An isotope is any of several different forms of a chemical element, each having different atomic mass. Fissionable isotopes are isotopes capable of nuclear fission. Nuclear fission is a process in which the nucleus of an atom splits into 2 or more smaller nuclei as fission products, releasing substantial amounts of useful energy and usually some by-product particles (e.g. 2 or 3 neutrons).

able for nuclear weapon production. U-235 is the only fissile isotope occurring in nature. Nuclear power plants utilize fission to produce electricity or heat.

Natural uranium contains 99.3 per cent of the isotope U-238 and 0.7 per cent of the fissionable isotope U-235. Uranium enrichment (the isotope separation process by which the abundance of a specified isotope in an element is increased) is a critical step in transforming natural uranium into nuclear fuel for use in a reactor to produce atomic energy.[22] Low-enriched uranium (LEU) contains between 0.7 and 20 per cent of U-235. Uranium can be used in many commercial nuclear reactors after having been enriched to between 3 and 5 per cent of U-235 but cannot be used in nuclear weapons at this level of enrichment. Highly enriched uranium (HEU) contains the isotope U-235 in a concentration above 20 per cent. HEU is used in research reactors and naval propulsion reactors and can also be used in nuclear weapons, for which it is usually enriched to around 90 per cent.

Plutonium is another heavy-metal element that is fissionable, and exists in more than one isotope. Virtually any combination of plutonium isotopes can be used to make a nuclear weapon but Pu-239 is preferred because others are unstable, less efficient or have a level of radioactivity that makes them difficult to handle. Pu-239 in metal form has been used in nuclear weapons, but plutonium dioxide is also used as a component of some nuclear fuels.

Pu-239 does not occur in nature but is produced in varying quantities during the nuclear reactions that take place in virtually all operating nuclear reactors. Spent nuclear fuel contains a small quantity of plutonium along with unused uranium and other highly radioactive fission products. In order to acquire Pu-239 in a form that can be used in nuclear weapons, a reprocessing plant is needed to carry out the chemical process of separating the plutonium from the other materials in spent fuel.

Pu-239, U-233, uranium enriched in the isotope 235 or 233, or any material containing one or more of the foregoing, are termed 'special fissionable material' by the IAEA.[23]

---

[22] Uranium can be used as fuel in certain types of reactor without enrichment. A 'self-sustaining fission chain reaction can be made in a reactor constructed from natural uranium and a suitable moderator, such as heavy water or graphite, alone'. Chemistry Division of the Los Alamos National Laboratory, 'Uranium', <http://pearl1.lanl.gov/periodic/elements/92.html>.

[23] IAEA (note 5), p. 31.

The nuclear fuel cycle

Generating atomic energy is dependent on a series of steps, often referred to together as the nuclear fuel cycle. The full nuclear fuel cycle consists of the mining of uranium, its processing to make it suitable for use in nuclear reactors, the 'burning' of the fuel in a reactor to produce electricity, the reprocessing of spent fuel and the subsequent final treatment of the waste products that remain after reprocessing.

Natural uranium is found all over the world in low concentrations. Uranium, once mined, is chemically treated to produce a concentrate known as yellowcake because of its distinctive colour. The yellowcake can be converted directly into uranium oxide, metal or the gaseous uranium hexafluoride, the feed material for uranium enrichment. The most common uranium enrichment processes are gaseous diffusion and centrifuge enrichment, although a number of other technologies have been developed. Enriched uranium hexafluoride is then converted into an oxide or other chemical compound and fabricated into the fuel, which most commonly takes the form of ceramic uranium dioxide pellets. These are packed into zirconium alloy tubes, which in turn are gathered into a fuel assembly that can be loaded into a reactor.

The fuel inside a reactor that undergoes the process of fission, which in turn generates atomic energy, must be replaced periodically. When the fuel is removed it needs to be stored for a period while the heat and radiation reduce to manageable levels, at which point it can be reprocessed, or sorted according to its level of radioactivity, stored and later disposed of.

Reprocessing is considered by many analysts to be a necessary and useful stage of the fuel cycle, although not all agree. During reprocessing it is possible to recover the remaining uranium and plutonium by separating them from the spent fuel. Recovered uranium can be manufactured into new fuel, while plutonium can be mixed with natural uranium to make a mixed oxide (MOX) fuel. Reprocessing is also said to dramatically reduce the volume of waste.

These points are disputed by other analysts. The cost–benefit assessment of reprocessing is influenced by the proliferation risks created by the separation of plutonium, which must be secured in the phase between separation and the fabrication of new fuel. Furthermore, reprocessing involves chopping spent fuel into small pieces that are then dissolved in acid. This procedure itself generates significant amounts of radioactive waste and, when this is offset against the reduction in mass from recovering reusable material, the benefits of reprocessing are less clear than its advocates suggest.

From this brief description it can be seen that some parts of the fuel cycle are of greater relevance than others in terms of nuclear weapon non-proliferation. In particular, mining and milling at the first stage of the cycle and the final disposal of radioactive waste from which uranium and plutonium have been removed have little relevance. Other parts of the nuclear fuel cycle make a more direct contribution to the production of special fissionable materials.

Weapon-grade uranium can be produced in the enrichment phase of the nuclear fuel cycle. The reprocessing phase leads to the recovery of plutonium. If the fuel is irradiated in the reactor for only a short period of time, the isotopic composition of plutonium recovered from such fuel is especially suitable for weapon production.

Few states possess either enrichment or reprocessing facilities. As the US ambassador to the Conference on Disarmament has noted:

International nuclear commerce has settled into a reliable system that provides reactors and fuel for NPT parties, with the vast majority of states foregoing the large economic and technical challenge of constructing their own
enrichment and reprocessing facilities. It is clear that the peaceful nuclear
benefits envisioned under the NPT can be fully realized without building an
enrichment or reprocessing plant.[24]

The following countries are all known to operate uranium enrichment facilities or to be in the process of building such facilities: Brazil, China, France, Germany, India, Iran, Japan, North Korea, the Netherlands, Pakistan, Russia, South Africa, the UK and the USA. Australia has developed laser enrichment technology but has not yet put it into commercial operation. Israel is strongly believed to have constructed a uranium enrichment facility at Dimona. In the 1980s Iraq began to acquire the technologies and equipment needed to build a uranium enrichment facility. Following the 1991 Gulf War IAEA inspectors found that Iraq had conducted enrichment experiments at a laboratory in Tuwaitha.

---

[24] United States Diplomatic Mission to the United Nations in Geneva, 'Statement by Ambassador Jackie W. Sanders, Permanent Representative, US Delegation to the Conference on Disarmament and Special Representative of the President for the Non-proliferation of Nuclear Weapons', 26 Feb. 2004, <http://www.usmission.ch/press2004/0226Sanders.htm>.

The following countries are known to currently operate spent-fuel reprocessing plants or reprocessing research projects: France, India, Israel, Japan, North Korea, Pakistan, Russia and the UK. A number of other countries (e.g. Argentina and Brazil) that have carried out research into reprocessing, including the construction of reprocessing facilities, have discontinued these activities.[25]

These lists of countries underline why such a close link has been drawn between the operation of uranium enrichment and spent-fuel reprocessing facilities and weapon capabilities. The correlation between possession of enrichment facilities, reprocessing facilities or both, on the one hand, and active efforts to develop nuclear weapons, on the other, is extremely strong. Through outreach and transparency initiatives the NSG has tried to combat the perception that one of its unstated objectives is to help existing nuclear powers to maintain their control over nuclear technologies (such as enrichment and reprocessing) for commercial rather than non-proliferation-related reasons. However, modern dual-use control lists include many items that may be nuclear-related but may also have other, non-nuclear applications, and there is suspicion that non-proliferation arguments are used to justify a de facto cartel that is lucrative for the nuclear industries of established nuclear powers. This is sometimes accompanied by the assertion that such control over key parts of the nuclear fuel cycle could be translated into political pressure by refusal to provide necessary materials and services or making access to them conditional on changes in behaviour.

II. The structure of the report

Chapter 2 describes the structure and the activities of the NSG and also considers its role and place in the overall context of nuclear non-proliferation treaties, agreements and processes. This consideration includes the relationship between the NSG and those provisions of the NPT that are relevant to export control.

Chapter 3 examines in more detail some of the main challenges to nuclear export control that have emerged in recent years and evaluates the possible role of the NSG in addressing these challenges. In this

---

[25] Feiveson, H. et al., 'Fissile materials: global stocks, production and elimination', *SIPRI Yearbook 2007: Armaments, Disarmament and International Security* (Oxford University Press: Oxford, 2007), pp. 558–76.

context it also considers two case studies of nuclear trade—those relating to India and Iran—in order to pinpoint some specific issues and problems in nuclear export control.

Chapter 4 examines several proposals and processes that have been launched recently in order to strengthen the NSG. This chapter also considers the implications for the NSG of other activities undertaken as part of the overall non-proliferation effort, including actions by the United Nations Security Council and actions by the IAEA. This includes identifying potential synergies and opportunities for cooperation as well as examining the risk for overlapping or redundant activities. The final chapter draws some conclusions from the discussion.

2. The structure and activities of the Nuclear Suppliers Group

I. The origins of the Nuclear Suppliers Group

The NSG is an informal arrangement in the sense that cooperation among the participants is not laid down in a binding instrument under international law.[26] The participating states have made a political commitment to implement two sets of guidelines—one for nuclear exports and the other for nuclear-related dual-use exports—through their national laws and administrative procedures. The 45 countries that participate also use the NSG as a mechanism through which they can exchange information on issues and developments of concern for nuclear proliferation.

The participating states view the NSG as an important and necessary supplement to international legal agreements such as the NPT and treaties that prohibit the presence of nuclear weapons in various parts of the world. The need for cooperation in nuclear export controls was already recognized at the time the NPT was being negotiated. The main purpose for this cooperation was to lay the foundation for a common interpretation of the central—yet ambiguous—provisions of the treaty. It was not, however, the NSG that was expected to lead in this work. Shortly after the NPT entered into force in 1970 a group of countries calling itself the Nuclear Exporters Committee began to meet to discuss export control-related issues emerging from ambiguities in the NPT. The objective of the discussions was to reach a common interpretation of the obligations stemming from the NPT in terms of what can legally be exported to countries that are not parties to the treaty. This body became known as the Zangger Committee after its first chairman—Claude Zangger.[27] The NSG, in contrast, aims to establish rules that also apply to states that are parties to the NPT.

---

[26] For a discussion of the formal nature of the cooperation within the NSG see Ahlström, C., *The Status of Multilateral Export Control Regimes: An Examination of Legal and Non-legal Agreements in International Cooperation* (Iustus Förlag: Uppsala, 2000).

[27] Additional information about the Zangger Committee is available at <http://www.zanggercommittee.org>. See also Schmidt, F. W., 'The Zangger Committee: its history and future role', *Nonproliferation Review*, no. 1, vol. 2 (fall 1994), pp. 38–44.

The Zangger Committee

The origin of the Zangger Committee can be traced to the lack of precision in the language of Article III.2 of the NPT. According to this provision, parties to the NPT undertake not to provide '(*a*) source or special fissionable material, or (*b*) equipment or material especially designed or prepared for the processing, use or production of special fissionable material', to any non-nuclear weapon state unless the source or special fissionable material is subject to IAEA safeguards. In practice, problems arose with the interpretation and definition of what constituted 'equipment or material especially designed or prepared for the processing, use or production of special fissionable material' (such material or equipment is commonly referred to as EDP, which stands for 'especially designed or prepared'). A further problem related to the conditions and procedures that would govern exports of EDP.

In order to reach a common understanding on these issues, a group of 15 states that were parties to the NPT, or were about to become parties to it, held a number of meetings in Vienna between 1971 and 1974. The importance of the matter cut across the East–West divide. Representatives of both Western democracies and Communist states participated in the formation of the Zangger Committee.

The main focus of the meetings was to find a solution that would comply with the obligation under Article III.2 while maintaining fair commercial competition between the parties to the NPT: uncertainties as to when safeguards are required could lead to different levels of competitiveness between exporters of nuclear technology in different countries.[28] By August 1974 the committee had reached two 'understandings' on the issues before it, the terms of which were specified in two memoranda. These memoranda sought to define source and special fissionable material and EDP, and set out controls governing their export. They form the basis for the Zangger Committee's guidelines today.

Memorandum A stated that the definitions of source and special fissionable material given in Article XX of the Statute of the IAEA[29]

---

[28] Fischer, D., 'The London Club and the Zangger Committee: how effective?', eds K. Bailey and R. Rudney, *Proliferation and Export Controls* (University Press of America: Lanham, Md., 1993), pp. 39–48.

[29] Statute of the IAEA, 23 Oct. 1956, <http://www.iaea.org/About/statute_text.html>.

would be used in relation to Article III.2 of the NPT. The memorandum also outlined the procedure to be followed when a party to the NPT exports such material to a non-nuclear weapon state not party to the NPT. Exporting states were to condition transfers on the requirement that source and special fissionable material would not be diverted for use in nuclear weapons or nuclear explosive devices and satisfy themselves that it would be subject to an IAEA safeguards agreement (i.e. where there is no requirement for 'full-scope' safeguards).[30] It also required exporting states to establish that recipients would not re-transfer material to a non-nuclear weapon state that is not a party to the NPT unless that state accepted IAEA safeguards.

Memorandum B contained a list defining the types of EDP that would 'trigger' IAEA safeguards—meaning that an item of EDP on the list could only be exported if the source or special fissionable material to be produced, processed or used in the EDP is subject to safeguards. The 'trigger list', as the memorandum became known, included items such as reactors and reactor equipment, as well as plants for the reprocessing of irradiated fuel elements. An annex appended to the list contained clarification of the different items listed. The members of the committee also agreed to exchange information on exports and export licences issued to any state not party to the NPT.[31] While the requirement in Article III.2 of the NPT not to export source or special fissionable material and EDP without safeguards applies in relation to *any* non-nuclear weapon state, the controls in memoranda A and B were limited to non-nuclear weapon states *not* party to the NPT.

Since its foundation, the Zangger Committee has kept the trigger list and its clarifications updated in light of developments in the field of nuclear technology. The adoption of these revisions and clarifications is decided by consensus within the committee and subsequently communicated to the IAEA. At a meeting in 1990 the committee decided that memoranda A and B would be redrafted in order to take into

---

[30] Safeguards are activities by which the IAEA can verify that a state is living up to its international commitments not to use nuclear programmes for nuclear weapon purposes. Full-scope safeguards are those activities that apply to all nuclear materials that could readily contribute to the development of nuclear weapons in a non-nuclear weapon state. For comprehensive definitions of IAEA safeguards and related topics see IAEA (note 5).

[31] IAEA, 'The Zangger Committee: a history 1971–1990', Annex to INFCIRC/209/Rev.1, Nov. 1990, p. 4.

account the amendments made; the resulting document was named the consolidated trigger list.[32]

Today there is a significant overlap between the export controls exercised under the Zangger Committee and part I of the NSG Guidelines, the only differences being the NSG's requirement for full-scope safeguards as a condition of supply and its controls over heavy water. Moreover, the participants in the two regimes are virtually the same.[33] This situation raises the question of whether or not it would be possible to amalgamate the two regimes into one. One argument in favour of such a development would be the rationalization of work. However, there are arguments of a political nature for maintaining the present order. As noted above, there is a clear link between the NPT and the Zangger Committee, and while the work of the committee has never been officially recognized by the other parties to the NPT as an authoritative interpretation of the treaty's provisions, they came close to such a recognition at the 2000 NPT Review Conference. In contrast, the likelihood of the NSG gaining recognition from the parties to the NPT is rather remote given its more controversial character (see the following discussion).

The formation of the NSG

The political salience of controls on nuclear technology transferred for peaceful purposes increased in 1974 when India (then, as now, a non-nuclear weapon state and not a party to the NPT) exploded a nuclear device.[34] This event prompted the UK and the USA to seek to strengthen the non-proliferation regime on nuclear weapons beyond the compass of the NPT and the Zangger Committee. A further incentive to strengthen the multilateral cooperation on export controls on

---

[32] For the latest version of the consolidated trigger list see IAEA, INFCIRC/209/Rev.2, 9 Mar. 2000.

[33] As of Sep. 2006, Belarus, Brazil, Cyprus, Estonia, Kazakhstan, Latvia, Lithuania, Malta and New Zealand participate in the NSG but not in the Zangger Committee. All Zangger Committee members participate in the NSG.

[34] Only those states that had exploded a nuclear explosive device before 1 Jan. 1967 and that are party to the NPT are recognized as 'nuclear weapon states' (i.e. China, France, Russia, the UK and the USA). All other states, including all states not party to the treaty, are defined as 'non-nuclear weapon states'. Thus, those states that possess nuclear weapons but are not party to the NPT (i.e. India, Israel, North Korea and Pakistan) are technically termed 'non-nuclear weapon states' because the NPT does not recognize their right to possess nuclear weapons. These states are commonly referred to as 'de facto nuclear weapon states'.

nuclear technology was the fact that important exporters of such technology remained at that time outside the NPT—and thus also outside the committee (e.g. France and Japan). In 1975 the UK, which was acting as a permanent secretariat of the Zangger Committee, invited six other nuclear suppliers—Canada, France, the Federal Republic of Germany, Japan, the Soviet Union and the USA—to a series of meetings in London at which the original guidelines were drafted. The guidelines were adopted in September 1977.[35]

Being an ad hoc arrangement, the nascent NSG was able to include states that were not parties to the NPT at that time. Moreover, because the discussions in the NSG were not directly associated with the text of the NPT, participating states were able to take a more flexible and extensive approach to developing a list of items subject to agreed guidelines. Furthermore, in contrast to the Zangger Committee controls, the NSG Guidelines apply to transfers to *all* non-nuclear weapon states (i.e. including those that are parties to the NPT).

At the same time, some parties to the NPT were concerned that the flexibility of the NSG could lead to excessive controls on nuclear technology that would undermine their right to develop peaceful uses of nuclear energy as set down in Article IV of the NPT.[36] Since most parties to the NPT had no nuclear weapon aspirations, they stressed the importance of ensuring that export controls did not reduce the prospects for economic development and free trade. After formulating the guidelines on nuclear transfers, the members of the NSG did not openly institutionalize the cooperation. The principal reason for this was the opposition it met among developing countries that saw the NSG, or the London Club as it was denominated then, as a 'supplier cartel, undermining the basis of the NPT's "bargain" between nuclear "haves" and "have-nots"'.[37] Although the group did not go on meeting, the guidelines adopted in the 1970s continued to influence the

---

[35] The guidelines were first published in Feb. 1978 as IAEA Document INFCIRC/254 and the IAEA has continued to publish the guidelines as subsequently amended.

[36] Article IV of the NPT states that 'All the Parties to the Treaty undertake to facilitate, and have the right to participate in, the fullest possible exchange of equipment, materials and scientific and technological information for the peaceful uses of nuclear energy. Parties to the Treaty in a position to do so shall also cooperate in contributing alone or together with other States or international organizations to the further development of the applications of nuclear energy for peaceful purposes, especially in the territories of non-nuclear-weapon States Party to the Treaty, with due consideration for the needs of the developing areas of the world.'

[37] van Ham, P., *Managing Non-Proliferation Regimes in the 1990s: Power, Politics and Policies* (Pinter Publishers: London, 1993), p. 16.

export policies of the members throughout the 1980s, and the members consulted with each other on a bilateral basis.

Events in the Gulf in the early 1990s prompted a revival of the multilateral cooperation within the NSG. In March 1991 the members of the NSG met in The Hague. Three main issues were on the agenda: (*a*) to update the trigger list in the light of developments in the field of nuclear technology, (*b*) the question of conditioning transfers with the acceptance of full-scope safeguards, and (*c*) the question of introducing controls on dual-use technology in the field of nuclear technology.

The three issues were settled at a meeting in Warsaw in March–April 1992. The 1977 guidelines were revised in order to take into account technical developments.[38] A further important achievement at the Warsaw plenary was that the NSG participants issued a statement in which they declared that full-scope safeguards would be required as a condition for future transfers.[39] The major development at the Warsaw meeting, however, was the adoption of the Guidelines for Transfers of Nuclear-Related Dual-Use Equipment, Material and Related Technology.[40] With remarkable speed, the working group established at the plenary in The Hague had succeeded in drawing up new guidelines on the exports of dual-use items. A significant weakness in the non-proliferation regime on nuclear weapons had hitherto been that the supply-side controls did not cover items that could be used for indigenous production of items on the trigger lists which—if they were to be exported from a state adhering to the supply-side controls—would be the object of safeguards. Furthermore, Article III.2 of the NPT applies to equipment and material especially designed or prepared for the processing, use or production of fissile materials. Hence, there are many dual-use goods and technologies relevant for a nuclear weapon acquisition programme that technically fall outside the scope of Article III.2.

---

[38] IAEA, Communications received from certain member states regarding guidelines for the export of nuclear material, equipment or technology, INFCIRC/254/Rev.1/Part 1, July 1992.

[39] IAEA, Statement on full-scope safeguards adopted by the adherents to the Nuclear Suppliers Guidelines: meeting of adherents to the Nuclear Suppliers Guidelines, INFCIRC/405, May 1992.

[40] IAEA, INFCIRC/254/Rev.1/Part 2 (note 38).

II. The NSG Guidelines

From its inception the NSG saw its activities as facilitating legitimate trade by reducing the risk that nuclear cooperation would contribute to nuclear proliferation. The view was that, without strengthened controls, nuclear trade for peaceful purposes could become politically unacceptable in some nuclear supplier states, thus putting their nuclear industries at a trading disadvantage without any advance with regard to non-proliferation.

For the most part the agreed guidelines have helped to establish a clear standard against which to judge applications to export trigger list items. This is intended to ensure predictability in the export licensing practices of participating states in order to reassure the nuclear industry (including both suppliers and recipients of controlled items) that non-proliferation policies are not a barrier to legitimate international nuclear trade.

At the same time, the criteria contained in the guidelines do not create any rights for exporters or importers and the NSG has also adopted a 'non-proliferation principle' whereby a supplier, notwithstanding provisions in the guidelines, should only authorize a transfer when it is satisfied that it would not contribute to the proliferation of nuclear weapons. This makes it clear that each decision rests with the responsible authorities in the exporting state and that factors such as adherence to the NPT do not alone guarantee nuclear supply.

Guidelines for nuclear transfers

NSG participating states make a political commitment to take into account two sets of agreed guidelines when making national decisions about exports of controlled items. Part I of the NSG Guidelines applies to the export of items that are defined by participating states to be exclusively for nuclear use. These items include: nuclear material; nuclear reactors and related equipment; non-nuclear material for reactors; plant and other equipment for the reprocessing, enrichment and conversion of nuclear material and for fuel fabrication and heavy water production; and technology associated with each of the above items.

The first set of guidelines for nuclear transfers, adopted in 1977, incorporated the NSG's own trigger list of items that were to be subject to the agreed rules. These guidelines require that exporters obtain formal government assurances from recipients stating that items on the trigger list will not be diverted to unsafeguarded nuclear fuel cycle or nuclear explosive activities. The guidelines also stipulate re-transfer provisions and require NSG participating states to exercise particular caution in the transfer of sensitive facilities, technology and weapon-usable materials.

The fact that the members of the NSG did not tie their activities directly to the provisions of the NPT facilitated agreement that the guidelines should be applied to transfers of trigger list items to all non-nuclear weapon states, regardless of whether they were party or not party to the treaty. On the other hand, it was the view of the Zangger Committee that states in compliance with the NPT should not be subject to conditions of supply and that common understandings could only apply to transfers to non-nuclear weapon states that were not party to the NPT.

At the same time, the original consensus guidelines agreed within the NSG were less restrictive than those proposed by some participants. In particular, proposals to require full-scope safeguards and international supervision of particularly sensitive (enrichment and reprocessing) facilities as conditions of supply were not acceptable to all participating states in 1977.[41]

At its meeting in Warsaw in 1992, the NSG agreed that the transfer of items in the NSG trigger list 'should not be authorised to a non-nuclear-weapon State unless that State has brought into force an agreement with the IAEA requiring the application of safeguards on all source and special fissionable material in its current and future peaceful nuclear activities'. This condition of supply did not prohibit transfers to non-nuclear weapon states without such a full-scope safeguards agreement, but the NSG stated that such transfers 'should only be authorised in exceptional cases when they are deemed essential for the safe operation of existing facilities and if safeguards are applied to those facilities'. Moreover, the guidelines were amended to urge that participating states 'should inform and, if appropriate, consult in the event that they intend to authorise or to deny such transfers'.[42]

---

[41] Thorne, C. E. (ed.), *A Guide to Nuclear Export Controls* (Proliferation Data Services: Burke, Va., 1997), p. 4.

[42] IAEA (note 39).

The original guidelines stated that agreements between suppliers and recipients should include provisions covering the reprocessing, storage, alteration, use, transfer or re-transfer of 'weapons-usable' material. In 2003, as a result of NSG discussions on how to reduce the risks of nuclear terrorism, this language was modified to apply to 'any material usable for nuclear weapons or other nuclear explosive devices'.

The language in the guidelines referring to controls on the re-transfer of trigger list items has also been strengthened over time. The guidelines suggest that any transfer should be accompanied by specific government-to-government assurances confirming that consent from the original supplier will be sought prior to any re-transfer of a trigger list item, or any controlled item that has been derived from the transfer of a trigger list item.

In 1994 the NSG added a provision (a non-proliferation principle) to part I of the guidelines, which currently states that 'notwithstanding other provisions of these Guidelines, suppliers should authorize transfer of items or related technology identified in the trigger list only when they are satisfied that the transfers would not contribute to the proliferation of nuclear weapons or other nuclear explosive devices or be diverted to acts of nuclear terrorism'. Carlton Thorne, a former chair of the Dual-use Working Group, has noted that the application of this provision introduced an element of subjectivity and judgement into part I of the guidelines; all the other provisions in part I can be said to be objective.[43] This guideline was amended in 2003, again in response to concerns about nuclear terrorism.

The guidelines for nuclear transfers also stress that NSG participating states should support activities that can enhance the effectiveness of export controls. One of the guidelines suggests that suppliers should promote international cooperation on physical protection measures (actions to help prevent the theft or illicit transfer of nuclear material and equipment), including physical security at nuclear installations, protection of nuclear materials in transit and measures to recover nuclear materials and equipment should they be lost or stolen. In 2003, again in response to concerns about nuclear terrorism, the NSG amended the guidelines to strengthen these measures.

The amended guidelines state that suppliers should promote adherence to international instruments, such as the 1980 Convention on the

[43] Thorne (note 41), Parts 1–6.

Physical Protection of Nuclear Material and Nuclear Facilities, and the widest possible adoption of the guidance and recommendations for the physical protection of nuclear material against theft developed by the IAEA.[44] In addition, the modified guidelines encourage suppliers to promote nuclear facility designs that enhance physical protection in ways that safeguard against terrorist attacks.

Guidelines for Transfers of Nuclear-related Dual-use Equipment, Materials, Software and Related Technology

Part I of the NSG Guidelines was elaborated in response to a political imperative created by a specific event—the testing of a nuclear explosive device by India in 1974. In 1991 a similar political imperative was created by the public disclosure of a clandestine nuclear weapon programme in Iraq. The programme had relied in part on the procurement of items that were not included on the trigger list or subject to the NSG Guidelines but that were then used by Iraq to build its own trigger list items.

Inspections carried out by the IAEA at nuclear installations in Iraq in the framework of UN Security Council Resolution 687[45] (that called for the elimination, under international supervision, of Iraq's nuclear, biological and chemical weapons, together with related items and production facilities) more fully revealed the extent of Iraq's programme and its procurement activities abroad. This gave major impetus to the NSG's development of dual-use guidelines.

The dual-use guidelines were developed in a working group established in January 1991 at an NSG meeting called by the government of the Netherlands. This was the first meeting of the NSG since the adoption of the original guidelines in 1977. The Dual-Use Working Group elaborated the guidelines at a series of meetings in 1991 and agreed them in January 1992. The NSG adopted the Guidelines for Transfers of Nuclear-related Dual-use Equipment, Material and Related Technology at its Warsaw plenary meeting in April 1992.[46]

---

[44] This guidance is published by the IAEA as 'The physical protection of nuclear material and nuclear facilities', INFCIRC/225/Rev.4 corrected, June 1999.

[45] UN Security Council Resolution 687, 3 Apr. 1991. Most UN documents can be accessed at <http://www.un.org/documents/>.

[46] These guidelines have since been updated and are now entitled Guidelines for Transfers of Nuclear-related Dual-use Equipment, Material, Sofware and Related Technology.

These dual-use guidelines also include a control list identifying the items to which they apply. The items on the control list are those that NSG participating states believe 'can make a significant contribution to an unsafeguarded nuclear fuel cycle or nuclear explosive activity, but which have non-nuclear uses as well, for example in industry'.[47]

The basic principle of the dual-use guidelines is that suppliers should not authorize transfers of controlled items if any of three conditions applies. The first condition applies when the item is for use in a non-nuclear weapon state in a nuclear explosive activity or an unsafeguarded nuclear fuel-cycle activity. While this condition refers only in cases of transfer to a non-nuclear weapon state, the other two conditions refer to any transfer. The second condition applies when there is an unacceptable risk of diversion to such activities. The third condition is when there is an unacceptable risk of diversion to acts of nuclear terrorism.

If none of these conditions applies, there is an assumption that the transfer will be authorized. To ensure that they are able to implement the basic principle in practice, suppliers should establish export licensing procedures. The dual-use guidelines include a list of factors that licensing officers should take into account when assessing whether or not to approve an application to transfer a controlled item. Some of these factors require licensing officers to assess information that is fairly easily obtained, such as whether or not the recipient country is party to one of a number of named international agreements and whether that country already has particularly sensitive facilities, such as a spent-fuel reprocessing plant.

However, to take into consideration other factors listed in the dual-use guidelines, licensing officers would need access to information that may be more difficult to come by. For example, it would require a technical evaluation to assess whether an item being exported is appropriate for its stated end-use and whether that use would be performed under normal circumstances. Also, to establish whether an end-user has ever engaged in questionable or illegal nuclear activities or been denied a licence by another supplier would call for the collection and storage of relevant data, including information gathered from other suppliers. Furthermore, to determine the level of risk that

---

[47] IAEA, 'The Nuclear Suppliers Group: its origins, role and activities', Attachment to communication received from the permanent mission of Australia on behalf of the member States of the Nuclear Suppliers Group, INFCIRC/539, 13 Sep. 1997.

an item will be diverted to acts of nuclear terrorism, licensing officers would require information from other authorities in their own country and from partner states.

In order to reduce the risk that dual-use items will be diverted from their authorized end-user or end-use after transfer, the dual-use guidelines include two conditions for transfer: provision of an end-user statement specifying the uses and location of use of the items and an explicit assurance that the items will not be used in ways inconsistent with the basic principle noted above. The dual-use guidelines also require the supplier to obtain assurances from the recipient that the items will not be re-transferred to a third country without prior consent from the responsible national authorities of the original supplier state. This assurance is only sought where the recipient is a state that does not adhere to the NSG Guidelines.

III. The structure of the Nuclear Suppliers Group

After 1977 the number of states adhering to the original guidelines for nuclear transfers grew steadily. The progressive expansion in the number of participating states is shown in table 2.1. In order to indicate their adherence to the guidelines, governments typically sent a letter to the IAEA Director General stating that from a specified date they were applying the measures contained in INFCIRC/254 through their national laws and administrative procedures. However, since the NSG adherents did not initially meet, the issue of membership of the NSG and what that might entail did not arise.

After 1991 the NSG began to meet regularly. It became necessary to think through such issues as who should meet, how the participants should conduct their business and whether (and under what conditions) new states should be allowed to engage in NSG activities.

The collective activities of the NSG consist today of a plenary meeting, a consultative group, information exchange meetings and ad hoc working groups organized to examine particular issues. The country acting as the NSG chair organizes the plenary meeting and coordinates activities for one calendar year. The chair can also be mandated to carry out activities on behalf of the group, such as outreach to particular countries to promote adherence to the NSG Guidelines. The NSG does not have a secretariat but the Japanese mission to the IAEA in Vienna has acted as an informal point of contact, greatly facilitating the administration of activities as well as communication and information exchange among participating states.

The NSG now holds a plenary meeting once a year. It also held an extraordinary plenary meeting in December 2002 to amend the guidelines in order to address the threat of nuclear exports being diverted to terrorism. The plenary meeting, which works by consensus, decides on revisions to the guidelines and the list of items subject to control, and agrees on activities to be carried out by or on behalf of the NSG. However, responsibility for implementing NSG decisions and carrying out agreed activities lies with the individual participating governments. The plenary can also decide to set up working groups of specialists to look in more detail at particular aspects of the guidelines, the technical annexes, procedural matters, information sharing and transparency activities. Immediately before each plenary there is an information exchange meeting at which participating states share information and discuss developments of relevance to the guidelines for nuclear transfer.

The consultative group, which works by consensus and consists of all participating states, is the NSG's deliberative body and meets at least twice annually. The group can also meet whenever it is considered necessary to discuss specific issues associated with the guidelines and the technical annexes.

The NSG has established the dual-use consultation body in response to the need for a mechanism to ensure the implementation of the dual-use guidelines. The body also serves as a forum for consultation and exchange of information on dual-use procurement activities of potential proliferation concern. It meets at least once a year and reports to the plenary. The body has its own chair which also rotates annually. The NSG established a separate Joint Information Exchange (JIE) for notifications related to transfers of dual-use equipment or technology. At the JIE, which immediately precedes the NSG plenary, participating states share information and discuss developments of relevance to the dual-use guidelines. Information is also exchanged on cases where licences to export dual-use items have been denied. To ensure that members do not approve transfers of dual-use items without first consulting with the state that issued the denial, the NSG adopted a so-called 'no undercut' principle at its meeting in Warsaw in 1992 as part of the memorandum of understanding on implementation of the

Table 2.1. Expansion of Nuclear Suppliers Group participation, 1977–2007

Year	Number of participants	States joining the NSG
1977	7	Canada, France, Federal Republic of Germany, Japan, UK, Soviet Union, USA
1982	17	Australia, Belgium, Czechoslovakia, German Democratic Republic, Finland, Italy, Netherlands, Poland, Sweden, Switzerland
1987	23	Bulgaria, Denmark, Greece, Hungary, Ireland, Luxembourg
1992	27[a]	Austria, Norway, Portugal, Romania, Spain
1997	34[b]	Argentina, Brazil, South Korea, New Zealand, South Africa, Ukraine
2002	40	Belarus, Cyprus, Kazakhstan, Latvia, Slovenia, Turkey
2004	44	China, Estonia, Lithuania, Malta
2005	45	Croatia
2007	45	

[a] In 1990 the Federal Republic of Germany and the German Democratic Republic were united and in 1991 Russia succeeded the Soviet Union in the NSG.
[b] In 1992 the Czech and Slovak Republics became separate members of the NSG.

Guidelines for Transfers of Nuclear-Related Dual-Use Equipment, Material and Related Technology.

According to this memorandum of understanding, the government of a nuclear supplier state should provide 'prompt notification to other Subscribing Governments of a decision it has made pursuant to the Guidelines not to authorize a transfer of equipment, material, or related technology identified in the Annex'. In turn, other governments:

should not authorize a transfer of equipment, material, or related technology identified in the Annex which is essentially identical to a transfer which was not authorized by another Subscribing Government ... without consulting the Subscribing Government which provided the notice. After such consultations, the Government, in the event of its authorization of the transfer, should notify other Subscribing Governments of its authorization. Thereafter the restriction on transfers set forth in the first sentence of this sub-paragraph will no longer apply.[48]

IV. Issues for the Nuclear Suppliers Group

Participation in the NSG

While it would be desirable for all states to adhere to the NSG Guidelines, based on past practice it appears that states are not invited to participate in the group. Instead, governments seeking to engage in NSG activities must make their wish known to the participating states, which then make a decision about whether or not to agree to this request. As decisions are taken by consensus, all NSG participating states must agree before a new government can join the group's activities. The NSG participating states have elaborated a number of factors that they will take into account in this connection. These factors include: (*a*) the ability to supply items (including items in transit) covered by the annexes to parts 1 and 2 of the NSG Guidelines; (*b*) adherence to the guidelines and action in accordance with them; (*c*) enforcement of a legally based domestic export control system that gives effect to the commitment to act in accordance with the guidelines; (*d*) adherence to one or more of the NPT, the treaties of Pelindaba, Rarotonga, Tlatelolco, Bangkok or an equivalent international nuclear non-proliferation agreement,[49] and full compliance with the obligations of such agreement(s); and (*e*) support of international efforts towards non-proliferation of weapons of mass destruction (WMD) and of their delivery vehicles.

One of the criteria appears to be particularly important. Today, countries that do not adhere to international nuclear non-proliferation agreements are excluded from participation in the NSG. This was not always the case: France, one of the states that founded the NSG in 1977, did not accede to the NPT until August 1992.

On other criteria there may be some flexibility. This is partly to avoid a 'catch-22' situation in which states are excluded from the NSG on the basis that they have not raised the level of their export

[48] NSG, Memorandum of understanding on implementation of the Guidelines for Transfers of Nuclear-Related Dual-Use Equipment, Material and Related Technology, Warsaw, Apr. 1992. Available at <http://web.sipri.org/contents/expcon/nsg_mou.html>.

[49] These treaties create nuclear weapon-free zones by specifying regions in which countries commit themselves not to manufacture, acquire, test or possess nuclear weapons.

controls to a standard that can in effect only be achieved through participation in the group. Flexibility also reflects the need for the NSG to address export control issues and problems in states that are not suppliers of controlled items but that are important transit or trans-shipment points. As these states are not themselves producers or suppliers of controlled items, they may not have detailed information about either product characteristics or end-users. Participation in information exchange processes is particularly critical if these countries are to implement effective controls. Access to the NSG information exchange is only possible through participation in the group.

All of the member states of the EU participate in the NSG, even if it can be questioned whether a number of them meet the established criteria listed above. Several EU member states neither supply items contained in the NSG control lists nor act as significant transit points. Moreover, there are EU member states that have little or no record of enforcement of a legally based export control system. However, all participate in the single market of the European Communities, meaning that most controlled items flow freely across their state borders. Furthermore, all are bound by the same primary legislation controlling dual-use exports, which is established in an EU Council Regulation. Therefore, if the overall NSG control system is not to be compromised, all member states need to apply the same criteria when evaluating export licence applications.

Once a state has met these criteria there is still no guarantee of participation, which requires a consensus decision by the NSG plenary. The NSG participating states have stressed that states can adhere to the guidelines (which are public documents) without joining the NSG.

At the 1995 NPT Review and Extension Conference the conference participants established a number of principles on non-proliferation and disarmament. One principle was that transparency in nuclear-related export controls should be promoted within the framework of dialogue and cooperation among all interested states party to the NPT. The NSG has subsequently organized two international seminars on the role of export controls in nuclear non-proliferation. The first seminar was held in 1997 at the IAEA in Vienna and the second was at the UN headquarters in New York in 1999. The NSG has also taken up various contacts and briefings with non-participating countries. In addition to the outreach activities conducted with potential members, the group conducts briefings of non-members with a view to increasing the understanding of and adherence to the guidelines.

In regard to the first factor noted above, a very wide spectrum of countries can supply controlled items, in particular those contained in the annex to the dual-use guidelines, which lists nuclear-related dual-use equipment, materials, software, and related technology. For example, the annex includes a range of machine tools and special metals that have non-nuclear applications.

Since the NSG Guidelines are implemented by each participating state in accordance with its national laws and practices, and decisions on export applications are taken at the national level in accordance with national export licensing requirements, the need for an effective national export control system is obvious. At the same time, there are no agreed standards that set out in detail the elements of a legally based domestic export control system.

It is widely recognized that three broad elements are required. First, primary and secondary legislation (such as laws, ordinances, decrees and regulations) must be adopted and in force to create the authorities necessary to support an effective system. Second, there must be institutions responsible for implementing this body of legislation by assessing transfers before controlled items leave the jurisdiction of the exporting state. These institutions must be provided with sufficient resources to carry out their allotted tasks, most likely to involve assessing and issuing export licences. Third, units and agencies within the law enforcement community must be empowered to enforce the legislation by carrying out investigations and, where necessary, prosecutions. These bodies also need to be provided with adequate knowledge and resources to carry out their duties.

Information exchange within the NSG

Two critical issues for the NSG are the questions of what information to share and how to share it. The development of national export control policies benefits from an exchange of ideas and from information about how other countries have addressed export control-related issues and problems. Licensing and enforcement officers benefit from information about new technical developments, about changes in the marketplace (such as the emergence of new transaction types and new means of technology transfer) and about the nature and activities of specific end-users.

These benefits create the demand for different kinds of information from the different parts of the export control community. Some of the information is openly available and can be freely shared. However, national legislation (including legislation related to privacy) also imposes limits on what each participating state can collect and share.

While information about specific exporters will be public after a case has been tried in court, states do not have a common approach to the publication or distribution of information about specific exporters during ongoing investigations prior to judicial proceedings. States also have different levels of sensitivity about exchanging or publishing information about nuclear developments in countries of concern or about particular end-users in foreign countries. Up to this point the NSG has not defined specific 'targets' for its activities—an issue discussed further in chapter 4.

The manner of information exchange has greatly altered with the development of new forms of electronic communication and the relative ease with which access to computerized databases can be shared. Traditional forms of information sharing such as bilateral diplomatic exchanges and direct contact between officials in bilateral or group meetings have been supplemented by automated systems.

Taken together, these developments have made it a complicated undertaking to ensure that those who enforce export controls have access to the information they need when they need it but do not receive irrelevant information or such a high volume of information that they are unable to process and absorb it.

As noted above, at various meetings NSG members already regularly exchange information on issues of nuclear proliferation concern and how these impact on national export control policy and practice. The Los Alamos National Laboratory in the USA has developed a secure networked database called the Nuclear Suppliers Group Information Sharing System (NISS). Within this system the national authorities of NSG participating states can share information in real time about movements of proliferation-sensitive equipment, materials and technology. In addition, information about denial actions by one state in the NSG can be disseminated rapidly to colleagues in other national authorities, reducing the possibility that an end-user can seek controlled items elsewhere.

Initial questions within the NSG about the security of this information system appear to have been addressed through experience of use. Any residual concerns seem to have been outweighed by the convenience of having access to such a system.

Issues and challenges

The expanded participation in the NSG may have created an additional complication for information exchange by increasing the reluctance of some states to share information among the wider circle of participants. A higher number of participants may escalate concerns about the security of confidential or secret information or that shared information will be used for commercial or political reasons rather than strictly for the purposes of the NSG.

Adapting the existing information exchange system (developed in the context of preventing the proliferation of nuclear weapons) to the needs of counterterrorism is likely to create additional challenges. Detailed information will be required about a more diverse range of individuals and other potential end-users in a much wider group of countries. Moreover, the quantities and types of item that could be subject to export controls may also be adapted in line with changing threat perceptions.

Another issue that has been raised in the context of export control information exchange is the need for better harmonization and communication among the multilateral export control regimes. Given the similarities in the lists of participating states, the development of separate but essentially parallel information and communication systems by the Australia Group, the Missile Technology Control Regime, the NSG and the Wassenaar Arrangement might be viewed as unnecessary and wasteful.[50] In this context many countries have expressed their support for the creation of a single, integrated database containing (at a minimum) regime documents and decisions, national point-of-contact information for licensing and enforcement, and information about denied parties, end-users and product classification. This system would allow a broad array of users to retrieve the information they need quickly.

---

[50] For recent developments in and background information on the various multilateral export control regimes see Anthony, I. and Bauer, S., 'Controls on security-related international transfers', *SIPRI Yearbook 2007* (note 25), pp. 641–47.

While the benefits of such a system are clear, questions about the level and conditions of access and participation (given the different membership of the various regimes), the legal status of the information in such a database and the cost of the administrative framework required to update and maintain the system have all proved to be stumbling blocks to its creation. Moreover, it can be argued that a harmonized list could mean that export licence applications are assessed without properly taking into account the specific context. In the case of nuclear, biological and chemical weapons, for example, not only is the nature of the controlled items different, but there are also significant differences in the identity and procurement behaviour of proliferators and in the level of danger posed by a failure to prevent proliferation.

Outreach to non-participating states

After the adoption in 2004 of UN Security Council Resolution 1540 on the proliferation of nuclear, biological or chemical weapons and their means of delivery, all states must implement effective export controls regardless of their participation in multilateral export control arrangements or in the NSG.[51]

A number of countries that do not participate in the NSG have the technical and industrial capacities to undermine the effectiveness of its activities should they emerge as nuclear suppliers. One potential response to this would be to expand participation in the NSG to cover as many of the global sources of supply of controlled items as possible. In this way a wider range of countries might benefit from the discussion of technical licensing and enforcement issues at what currently represents the highest international standard. Moreover, in time a process of socialization might lead countries to adopt the standards and norms shared by most NSG participating states.

However, this approach is not supported by some NSG participants that believe that only those countries willing to accept a shared normative framework should join. Therefore, although the number of states in the NSG has grown over time, the criteria established by existing participants effectively limit future expansion.

The NSG has undertaken outreach activities to try to encourage as many states as possible to adhere to its guidelines, to put in place and

[51] UN Security Council Resolution 1540, 28 Apr. 2004.

enforce law-based national export controls and to support international non-proliferation efforts. The NSG outreach programme has included regular contacts with specific countries to inform them about NSG practices and to promote adherence to the guidelines. These contacts have taken place both through the activities of the NSG chair and through dialogue with non-participating states in the margins of international meetings such as the IAEA General Conference.

The NSG and IAEA safeguards

As noted above, the NSG Guidelines make specific reference to the technical measures, known as safeguards, that the IAEA has developed to verify declarations by states about their nuclear material holdings. These technical measures are intended to detect any diversion of declared nuclear material.

Nuclear export controls have been most directly connected to those full-scope IAEA safeguards that apply to 'all source or special fissionable material in all peaceful nuclear activities' within the territory of a non-nuclear weapon state by virtue of participation in the NPT.[52] The IAEA verifies a state's holdings of nuclear material by collecting information through declared information and inspections. The IAEA evaluates whether the information declared by states is internally consistent, consistent with information available from inspections and consistent with information available to the IAEA from other sources.

A full-scope safeguards evaluation allows the IAEA to reach a conclusion on whether declared nuclear material has been diverted from its stated end-use. On the basis of what is declared or known about nuclear activities (such as design information and operating records from reactors, inspection data or environmental samples taken by inspectors) the IAEA can judge if the amount of nuclear material that a state has declared is too low.

Full-scope safeguards do not verify the completeness of declarations by states, nor are they designed to uncover undeclared activities. However, the bilateral agreements that detail the safeguards to be applied in a country should contain provision for 'special inspections' by the IAEA if it considers that information made available by a state (e.g. through official explanations and routine inspections) is not

---

[52] These have been elaborated in a model agreement. See IAEA, INFCIRC/153 (Corrected), June 1972.

adequate for the agency to fulfil its responsibilities.[53] The conclusions reached on the basis of full-scope safeguards by the IAEA are a useful indicator of whether a state takes seriously its nuclear non-proliferation commitments and obligations. However, in the early 1990s it was recognized that further measures would be needed to complement this form of nuclear material accounting if the IAEA was to play its full role in assuring peaceful use of nuclear technology.

One approach that could extend the coverage of safeguards would be to insist that so-called 'facility-specific safeguards' must apply at all nuclear installations in a country. Facility-specific safeguards, which are developed in bilateral agreements between states and the IAEA, take into account security aspects of facility design and physical protection of materials, whereas full-scope safeguards focus on fissile material as it flows through the nuclear fuel cycle.[54] However, facility-specific safeguards have largely fallen into disuse with the more widespread application of full-scope safeguards and the subsequent development of a new IAEA instrument called the Additional Protocol.

The Additional Protocol

The effort to strengthen safeguards in order to detect undeclared activities, and to monitor the completeness as well as the correctness of state declarations, led to the IAEA '93 + 2' programme to develop a new model agreement.[55] This in turn led to the creation of the Additional Protocol—an addition to safeguards agreements between individual states and the IAEA. Countries that sign an Additional Protocol undertake to provide a range of information about their national nuclear activities to supplement that required under their full-scope

---

[53] IAEA (note 52), para. 73.

[54] In 2004 Matthew Bunn observed that facility-specific safeguards 'cover both facilities and material, and are not limited primarily to agreed strategic points, so that for those facilities and materials that are covered, safeguards can be more comprehensive'. Bunn, M., 'Lecture notes: international safeguards: summarizing "traditional" and "new" measures', Massachusetts Institute of Technology OpenCourseWare, <http://ocw.mit.edu/>.

[55] Programme 93 + 2 (which was launched in 1993 and was to make recommendations within 2 years) sought to bring about comprehensive reform of the safeguards system to improve the effectiveness and efficiency of safeguards. This effort was largely a result of the failure to detect Iraq's nuclear weapon programme, which was exposed after the 1991 Gulf War. See Walker, W., 'Reflections on transparency and international security', ed. N. Zarimpas, SIPRI, *Transparency in Nuclear Warheads and Materials: The Political and Technical Dimensions* (Oxford University Press: Oxford, 2003), p. 22.

safeguards, which remain in force. The type of information to be reported is negotiated between the IAEA and individual states and might include: a description of nuclear fuel cycle-related research and development activities (including any that are funded, specifically authorized or controlled by, or carried out on behalf of the state concerned but outside its territory); a description of the scale of operations of each location engaged in manufacturing activities; information regarding uranium mines and concentration plants and about the quantities and location of stocks of uranium ore and concentrates; information regarding locations with certain quantities of specified nuclear materials as well as about exports and imports of certain quantities of these materials; information regarding the location or further processing of intermediate or high-level waste containing plutonium, highly enriched uranium or U-233; information on specified equipment and non-nuclear material (including exports and imports of such items); and information regarding general plans for the next 10-year period relevant to the development of the nuclear fuel cycle.

The Additional Protocol, once in force, gives the IAEA greater rights of access to declared facilities, sites and locations. The agency decides on the structure of the inspection regime (i.e. the location and frequency of visits) needed to provide assurances that the declaration is complete. The protocol also permits the agency to inspect any location (declared or not) to investigate questions or inconsistencies in a national declaration.

An Additional Protocol in combination with full-scope safeguards (known as 'integrated safeguards') is intended to provide 'as complete a picture as practicable' of the production and holdings of nuclear source material, 'the activities for further processing of nuclear material (for both nuclear and non-nuclear application), and of specified elements of the infrastructure that directly support the state's current or planned nuclear fuel cycle'. Moreover, the increased access for inspectors is intended 'to help assure that undeclared nuclear activities are not concealed within declared nuclear sites or at other locations where nuclear material is present. Inspection mechanisms are also provided for instances where there appear to be inconsistencies between all information available to the agency and the declaration made by States regarding the whole of their nuclear programme'.[56]

[56] Rockwood, L., 'The model Additional Protocol: a contribution to global non-proliferation objectives', IAEA Regional Seminar on the Protocol Additional to Nuclear Safe-

The Additional Protocol as a potential condition of supply

The combination of full-scope safeguards and an Additional Protocol should further raise the level of confidence that a state is engaged solely in peaceful nuclear activities.[57] This higher level of confidence has clear benefits for export control authorities in nuclear supplier states when they are assessing applications to export controlled items.

As noted above, in 1992 the NSG agreed to adopt full-scope safeguards as a condition of supply. The 1995 NPT Review and Extension Conference endorsed this decision by agreeing a set of Principles and Objectives for Nuclear Non-Proliferation and Disarmament. One of these agreed principles was that:

new supply arrangements for the transfer of source or special fissionable material or equipment or material especially designed or prepared for the processing, use or production of special fissionable material to non-nuclear weapon states should require, as a necessary precondition, acceptance of the agency's full-scope safeguards and internationally legally binding commitments not to acquire nuclear weapons or other nuclear explosive devices.[58]

Since the introduction of the Additional Protocol in 1997, proposals have been put forward to introduce a new condition of supply in the NSG requiring recipients to bring an Additional Protocol into force before receiving controlled items. Could the NSG lead the way in this respect as it did in establishing full-scope safeguards as a condition of supply? This standard would probably increase the number of licence denials. The proposal made by President Bush that integrated safeguards should become a condition of supply for NSG participating states would maintain the connection between nuclear export controls and the safeguards system. However, this proposal is difficult to reconcile with other US proposals to the NSG, such as the creation of a special status for India.[59]

guards Agreements, Lima, Peru, 4–7 Dec. 2001, <http://www.opanal.org/Articles/safeguards/safeguards.html>.

[57] For more on the development of integrated safeguards see IAEA, Background on IAEA Board of Governors' framework for integrated safeguards, <http://www.iaea.org/News Center/News/2002/sgarticle_02.shtml>.

[58] 'Principles and objectives for nuclear non-proliferation and disarmament', NPT/CONF.1995/32 (Part I), 17 Apr–12 May 1995, <http://disarmament.un.org/wmd/npt/1995 nptrevconf.html>.

[59] On Indian–US nuclear cooperation see chapter 3 in this volume, section II; and Ahlström, C., 'Legal aspects of the Indian–US Civil Nuclear Cooperation Initiative', *SIPRI*

According to a statement by NSG members, 'few NPT parties have been refused controlled items: this has occurred when a supplier had good reason to believe that the item in question could contribute to nuclear proliferation. Almost all rejections by NSG members of applications for export licences have concerned states with unsafeguarded nuclear programmes'.[60]

As of 25 August 2006 there were 42 non-nuclear weapon states party to the NPT that had not yet brought into force a full-scope safeguards agreement with the IAEA. These states already fail to meet existing NSG conditions of supply. However, in most cases they are countries with few, if any, nuclear activities and therefore do not form part of the international market for controlled nuclear items. As of June 2007, 112 countries had signed an Additional Protocol to their full-scope safeguards agreement but 30 of these countries have not yet brought it into force. Moreover, several NSG participating states are among them, namely Argentina, Belarus, Brazil, Russia and the USA. Of these countries, Argentina and Brazil have not taken any steps to conclude such an agreement with the IAEA.

Use of the Additional Protocol as a condition of supply might, depending on how it was applied, encourage more states to put in place agreements with the IAEA. The prospect of losing access to controlled items (possibly including nuclear-related dual-use items for non-nuclear purposes) from NSG participating states might be a powerful incentive. However, it could be difficult to secure unanimous agreement to adopt this strict conditionality and, even if an attempt was successful, the approach might carry risks.

It should also be noted that the requirement for full-scope safeguards as a condition of supply has become somewhat controversial within the NSG itself (see the discussion in chapter 3 on Russia's trade with India). Hence, it certainly cannot be taken for granted that it will be possible to muster the necessary support within the NSG for an amendment of the requirement from the INFCIRC/153 standard of 1972 to the level outlined in INFCIRC/540 of 1997.[61]

Furthermore, adopting such a requirement might also have negative consequences. A number of countries (notably Japan) have invested

---

Yearbook 2006: Armaments, Disarmament and International Security (Oxford University Press: Oxford 2006).

[60] IAEA, INFCIRC/539, 16 Sep. 1997.

[61] IAEA (note 52); and IAEA, INFCIRC/540, Sep. 1997.

significant resources in persuading countries to agree to an Additional Protocol using the argument that there is a strong mutual interest in strengthening global non-proliferation efforts. The Additional Protocol is presented by Japan as an instrument to develop a nuclear non-proliferation culture under multilateral auspices. While the responses of states to these efforts at persuasion appear to have been largely positive, it is uncertain how countries would respond if elements of conditionality and coercion were introduced in parallel.

There may also be a risk that importers will turn to new suppliers from outside the NSG participating states to meet their needs, or develop and produce the items in question themselves. If this was to occur, then denial of access could disadvantage existing exporters in NSG participating states and multiply the sources of supply without achieving any non-proliferation benefit. Moreover, if the guidelines led to the denial of exports that were clearly not for a nuclear end-use or exports that posed no proliferation risk, this would undermine the NSG's argument that the arrangement was not a restrictive trade practice. Denials of this kind might also lead exporters to challenge the legality of denial decisions under national export laws.

Full-scope safeguards are an indicator of whether a state takes seriously its nuclear non-proliferation commitments and obligations. Conversely, a statement by the IAEA that a state had failed to comply with the provisions of a safeguards agreement can be interpreted as a warning signal. A decision by NSG participating states not to authorize exports to any state whose compliance with the letter or spirit of full-scope safeguards has been found unsatisfactory by the IAEA Director General or Board of Governors would seem reasonable.

The questions raised about the future effectiveness and activities of the NSG are difficult to examine as abstract propositions. Chapter 3 examines how some of the issues surrounding the NSG Guidelines have been discussed in the context of nuclear supply arrangements with two particular countries: India and Iran.

3. The impact of the NSG Guidelines on national export licensing

I. Introduction

The NSG does not take decisions about individual export transactions. The decision to approve a particular transaction is taken by the participating state concerned under the legal authority of its national laws and regulations. However, these national decisions are supposed to be consistent with the commitments that all participating states have made through the decisions of the NSG.

Export licensing helps not only to implement the political decisions taken by states in the NSG, but also to assure that the legal obligations contained in bilateral nuclear cooperation agreements between governments are respected. These legal commitments may derive from decisions taken in the NSG that have subsequently been woven into bilateral agreements.

For example, since 1974 Canada has required a government-to-government nuclear cooperation agreement before it will consider the export of any controlled item to a non-nuclear weapon state. In these agreements, which are only concluded with countries that are party to the NPT (and that therefore accept full-scope safeguards), Canada's partners provide a range of assurances related to non-proliferation. A number of these assurances mirror elements that are contained in the NSG Guidelines. The nuclear cooperation partners of Canada give assurances: (*a*) that Canadian nuclear exports will be used only for peaceful, non-explosive end-uses; (*b*) that Canada will have control over the re-transfer to a third party of any Canadian items subject to a nuclear cooperation agreement; (*c*) that Canada will have control over the reprocessing of any Canadian spent nuclear fuel and over the storage and subsequent use of any separated plutonium; (*d*) that Canada will control the enrichment of Canadian uranium and the subsequent storage and use of the highly-enriched uranium; (*e*) that, in the event the IAEA is unable to apply safeguards in the partner country, Canada will be permitted to carry out bilateral safeguards; and (*f*) that adequate physical protection measures will be taken with respect to Canadian nuclear items so as to ensure that they will not be stolen or otherwise misused.[62]

While the NSG Guidelines specify factors that national authorities should take into account when making their decisions, states are not barred from imposing additional conditions and guidelines based on their national requirements and policy preferences. Moreover, the factors taken into account during licensing need not only reflect non-proliferation objectives. As Carlton Thorne has observed, 'a supplier state may wish to control nuclear-related commodities and technologies to some states on the basis of their conduct in areas such as human rights, or their association with terrorist activities, or for any other reasons where trade controls or sanctions are chosen to make a point of principle'.[63] While these types of foreign policy controls may be required by national imperatives, they are not reflected in the decisions of the NSG, which are clearly linked to the objective of nuclear non-proliferation.

Within the EU, member states are legally obliged to apply the NSG Guidelines in the framework of the common dual-use export control system established under EU law. Article 8 of the Council Regulation that established the system states that 'in deciding whether or not to grant an export authorization under this Regulation, the Member States shall take into account all relevant considerations including . . . the obligations and commitments they have each accepted as a member of the relevant international non-proliferation regimes and export control arrangements'.[64]

In the light of the NSG Guidelines, the main factors that would need to be considered in reviewing applications for licences are: (*a*) the stated end-use of the item and whether it is consistent with what is known about the actual end-use; (*b*) the significance for nuclear purposes of the particular item (including both an evaluation of its technical characteristics and its availability elsewhere); (*c*) the types of nuclear non-proliferation assurances or guarantees given in a particular case; and (*d*) the non-proliferation credentials of the recipient country.

---

[62] Canadian Nuclear Association, 'Nuclear facts: does Canada contribute to nuclear weapons proliferation?', <http://cna.ca/english/facts.asp>.

[63] Thorne (note 41).

[64] Council Regulation (EC) no. 1334/2000 (note 9), Article 8.

II. Nuclear supplies to India: issues for the Nuclear Suppliers Group

The NSG owes its existence to the test of a nuclear explosive device by India in May 1974. Ironically, India did not object to the NSG Guidelines for Nuclear Transfers when they were first formulated because of the failure to agree on a proposal that full-scope safeguards should become a condition of supply at that time. India already applied other types of safeguards—so-called facilities safeguards—at some locations and so was able to meet the original conditions of supply.

The 1992 revision of the NSG Guidelines introduced the requirement that IAEA full-scope safeguards be applied to all current and future nuclear activities as a condition for all significant new nuclear exports to non-nuclear weapon states. This was a change that had great potential importance for India's relations with nuclear suppliers.

On 27 March 1992 President of the Russian Federation Boris Yeltsin signed Decree no. 312, which embedded the new NSG requirement in Russian law. Since then significant new nuclear exports from Russia to India have been prohibited with one exception. Russia has the right to build two nuclear reactors at the nuclear power plant in Kudankulam, located in Tamil Nadu in southern India.[65] A formal agreement to sell these reactors was signed four years before the change was made in the NSG Guidelines and therefore qualifies as a 'grand-fathered activity'. While the full-scope safeguards requirement does not apply to agreements or contracts drawn up on or prior to 3 April 1992,[66] negotiations on the construction of Russian nuclear reactors in Kudankulam began in 1979. The agreement was signed in New Delhi on 20 November 1988 by Soviet President Mikhail Gorbachev and Indian Prime Minister Rajiv Gandhi.[67]

---

[65] For details see Fedchenko, V., 'O nekotorykh aspektakh Rossiisko-Indiiskogo sotrud-nichestva v oblasti mirnoi yadernoi énergetiki' [On some aspects of Russian–Indian cooper-ation in the field of nuclear power engineering], *Yaderny Kontrol*, no. 3 (May/June 2001), <http://www.pircenter.org/data/publications/yk3-2001.pdf>, pp. 62–73.

[66] IAEA, INFCIRC/254/Rev.6/Part 1 (note 8), May 2003, para. 4(c).

[67] Fedchenko, V., Shilin, A. and Timerbaev, R., 'Russian–Indian nuclear relations and export control issues', *The Problem of Proliferation and Non-proliferation in South Asia: Current Situation and Perspectives*, PIR Study Paper no. 17 (PIR Center: Moscow, 2001), <http://www.pircenter.org/english/science/about.htm>, pp. 63–65; and 'Indo-Soviet Agree-ment signed', *Nuclear Engineering International*, Jan. 1989, p. 2.

The NSG Guidelines state that transfers to a non-nuclear weapon state without full-scope safeguards may be authorized in exceptional cases when they are 'deemed essential for the safe operation of existing facilities and if safeguards are applied to those facilities'.[68] Decree no. 312 did not mention any exceptions to the requirement for full-scope safeguards, but on 7 May 2000 soon after the inauguration of President Vladimir Putin, it was amended to introduce a safety-related exception, adjusting Russian legislation in accordance with the existing NSG Guidelines. This adjustment later became the basis for a dispute related to Russian nuclear fuel supply to the Tarapur nuclear power plant.[69]

The Tarapur plant was built by US companies in the late 1960s. However, after 1974 the USA refused to continue supplying fuel for the reactor and India began buying fuel from France. Shipments of French fuel continued until 1991 when France decided to sell nuclear fuel only to states where full-scope safeguards were in place. Left without a supplier, India began negotiations with China and reached agreement in 1995—at a time when China was not a member of the NSG and not obliged to require full-scope safeguards as a condition for supply. However, after India carried out new nuclear tests in 1998 China refused to continue supplies. India once again had to find a new source of fuel.

India approached Russia, and on 16 August 2000 an agreement was reached that JSC Mashinostroitelny Zavod—a nuclear fuel-producing engineering plant in Elektrostal, Moscow oblast—would supply approximately 58 tonnes of 1.66–2.6 per cent enriched uranium dioxide pellets. The Russian Ministry of Atomic Energy (Minatom) claimed that this agreement was justified under the safety-related exception envisaged in the NSG Guidelines and codified in the amended Decree no. 312. Supply began in mid-February 2001 and was strongly criticized by the USA and other NSG members (with the exception of Belarus).[70] This criticism was rebuffed by Minister of Atomic Energy Evgeny Adamov, who publicly hinted that Moscow

---

[68] IAEA, INFCIRC/254/Rev.6/Part 1 (note 66), para. 4(b).

[69] Fedchenko, Shilin and Timerbaev (note 67), p. 74–76.

[70] Fedchenko (note 65), p. 67. See e.g. US Department of State, 'Russian shipment of low enriched uranium fuel to India', Press release, 16 Feb. 2001, <http://www.state.gov/r/pa/prs/ps/2001/592.htm>.

could withdraw from the NSG if the group continued to cause problems for Russia's nuclear trade.[71]

Other elements in overall Indo-Russian nuclear cooperation are continuing but raise different questions than the deal in Tarapur. Russia will provide India with nuclear reactors and train personnel to operate the Kudankulam plant and will also guarantee the supply of nuclear fuel for the reactors.[72] Based on its experience with Tarapur, the Indian Government will ensure that any nuclear reactor will have a substantial reserve of fuel to minimize the risks associated with dependence on foreign supplies. In 1988, when the intergovernmental agreement on the Kudankulam nuclear power plant was signed, it was envisaged that spent nuclear fuel would be returned to the Soviet Union for reprocessing. Under the current arrangement, however, the spent nuclear fuel will remain in India as the property of the Atomic Energy Commission of India under IAEA safeguards.

Nuclear cooperation with India: future prospects

In June 2006 S. K. Jain, chairman and managing director of the Nuclear Power Corporation of India Limited (NPCIL), announced in an interview that India is prepared to import more nuclear reactors from France, Russia and the USA, and named Japan as a fourth potential supplier. The NPCIL prefers to set up reactors of the same type and from the same country at any given site. Jain stated that the Kudankulam site has been assessed as capable of hosting eight Russian VVER-1000 reactors in total, and that sites for French and US reactors would be prepared and reserved before the end of 2006.[73] Recent developments suggest that France, Russia and the USA are willing to supply reactors to India: all three countries have a strong

---

[71] Radyuhin, V., 'India, Russia nuclear cooperation will continue', *The Hindu*, 17 Dec. 2000.

[72] The Russian nuclear fuel company TVEL and the NPCIL signed a $400 million contract on 12 Feb. 2003 to provide Kudankulam with fuel until 2010. However, under the agreement fuel supplies will continue for the entire lifespan of the plant. 'India: Russian company to provide fuel for Kudankulam', Global Security Newswire, 14 Feb. 2003, <http://www.nti.org/d_newswire/issues/2003/2/14/5p.html>; and Radhakrishnan, R. K., 'Fuel supply agreement with Russia for Koodankulam', *The Hindu*, 22 Mar. 2003, <http://www.thehindu.com/2003/03/22/stories/2003032203471100.htm>.

[73] Subramanian, T. S., 'Working to a plan: interview with S. K. Jain, Chairman and Managing Director of Nuclear Power Corporation of India Limited', *Frontline*, 3–16 June 2006, <http://www.hinduonnet.com/fline/fl2311/stories/20060616001909200.htm>.

interest in re-evaluating the future relationship between India and the NSG.

The Russian Federation

India is planning a significant expansion of its nuclear power industry and the mutual interest of India and Russia to maintain and expand nuclear cooperation beyond Kudankulam is obvious. The Soviet Union had announced its readiness to share its experience of nuclear power plant construction with India as far back as in 1955, only a year after the world's first plant was commissioned in Obninsk, and during the 1990s (when there was almost no internal demand for new nuclear power equipment in Russia) exports to India helped the Russian nuclear power industry to survive.[74] The construction and modernization of new nuclear power plants abroad is one of the few dynamic parts of Russia's manufacturing industry.

For India, external assistance in the construction of nuclear power plants is crucial if it is to meet its targets for nuclear power generation, and Russia has agreed to finance 85 per cent of the cost of construction at Kudankulam using long-term loans. In India, modern reactors, like the Russian VVER-1000, are considered to be a catalyst for growth in other high-technology areas, as well as an essential driver for increasing per capita consumption of electricity in order to raise the quality of life of the population.

Support from President Putin has given momentum and substance to the cooperation. As noted above, Russian export control legislation was slightly modified by an amendment to Decree no. 312 soon after Putin's inauguration in May 2000. A few months later, in his address to the Millennium Summit in New York on 6 September, President Putin called for a global initiative to develop new nuclear power-production technology.[75] In his speech Putin asserted that the policies of restricting nuclear technology transfers to other countries and

---

[74] Kozlov, V., 'Perspectives on Russian atomic export', *Yaderny Kontrol*, vol. 9, no. 3 (fall 2003), <http://www.pircenter.org/data/publications/yk3-2003.pdf>, p. 119.

[75] President of the Russian Federation Vladimir V. Putin, Address to the Millennium Summit, United Nations, New York, N.Y., 6 Sep. 2000, <http://www.un.org/millennium/webcast/statements/russia.htm>.

enhanced international control have proved to be insufficient barriers to nuclear proliferation.[76]

One month later, during President Putin's visit to India the Vice-Prime Minister of the Russian Federation and the Principal Secretary to the Prime Minister of India signed a memorandum of Understanding (MOU) on intensifying bilateral cooperation in the peaceful uses of atomic energy. The text of this MOU was never made public, but press accounts assert that 'at the heart of this path-breaking agreement is a Russian commitment to contribute to India's growing nuclear energy requirements' in a manner that fully respects the country's international legal obligations on transfer of nuclear technology.[77]

Shortly after his appointment as Russia's Atomic Energy Minister in March 2001, Alexander Rumyantsev reiterated the commitment to continue nuclear cooperation with India. In the same announcement Rumyantsev noted the problem that, under the NSG Guidelines, Russia was restricted in its ability to supply new nuclear reactors to India, which continues to refuse to place all its nuclear facilities under full-scope safeguards. However, Rumyantsev expressed his confidence that 'some sort of memorandum' could be agreed within the NSG to facilitate peaceful Russian nuclear cooperation with India.[78] This arrangement would need to assign India a special status in regard to the NSG Guidelines.[79] In 2000–2001 Russia is reported to have proposed that India become an 'associate member' of the NSG but received 'a very negative response'.[80] In a press statement after its plenary meeting in Aspen, Colorado, on 10–11 May 2001, the NSG

---

[76] Concerning the Initiative of the President of the Russian Federation on energy supply for sustained development of mankind, radical solution of problems posed by proliferation of nuclear weapons, and global environmental improvement, announced at the UN Millennium Summit on 6 Sep. 2000.

[77] Raja Mohan, C., 'Putin strikes a nuclear deal', *The Hindu*, 5 Oct 2000, <http://www.hindu.com/2000/10/05/stories/01050002.htm>.

[78] Radyuhin, V., 'Russia to continue nuclear cooperation with India', *The Hindu*, 18 Apr. 2001, <http://www.hindu.com/2001/04/18/stories/03180005.htm>.

[79] The Russian Ministry for Atomic Energy has put forward 3 arguments in support of the need to treat India as a special case. First, since India has developed its own nuclear weapon technologies the NSG Guidelines do not make a direct impact on Indian capabilities. Second, India has a flawless record on nuclear non-proliferation. Third, India has no alternative to nuclear power to meet its energy needs and will find its economic development adversely affected unless it gains greater access to the international nuclear-power trade. See Radyuhin, V., 'Russia for lifting ban on nuclear deals with India', *The Hindu*, 3 Nov. 2003, <http://www.hindu.com/2003/11/03/stories/2003110304141200.htm>.

[80] Fedchenko, Shilin and Timerbaev (note 67), p. 14; and Baruah, A. and Ramachandran, R., 'Russian fuel for Tarapur ruled out', *The Hindu*, 6 Dec. 2004.

agreed to 'consider options for engaging with non-NSG countries that have developed nuclear programs and that are potential nuclear suppliers, for the purpose of strengthening the global nuclear non-proliferation regime'.[81]

In December 2002, answering a journalist's question about the possible supply of additional nuclear reactors to India, President Putin stated that Russia works within the framework of international rules and obligations and continues to meet its obligations, but that all the rules and regulations require improvement—including those in the nuclear sphere.[82] After the NSG plenary meeting in Busan, South Korea, on 22–23 May 2003 the Russian Ministry of Foreign Affairs released a press statement noting that 'the activities of the NSG should not, of course, create obstacles for international cooperation in the field of peaceful use of atomic energy and take into account new realities in this field in an adequate and timely manner'.[83]

During the visit to Russia of Indian Prime Minister Atal Bihari Vajpayee in November 2003, Rumyantsev stated that Russia would continue to push for lifting international restrictions on the flow of nuclear technologies to India. He said that 'it is high time to review bans on nuclear cooperation with India imposed in 1992 by the Nuclear Suppliers Group' and to work out a special arrangement to allow India to cooperate with other countries in the nuclear field.[84] Minatom was willing to pursue even quite exotic options to circumvent NSG regulations. In November 2003 Russia made a proposal to India for the construction of floating nuclear power plants, which had been developed in Russia but never built. The project would involve bringing the floating reactors close to Indian shores manned with a Russian crew and then selling the electricity generated to India, thus avoiding the NSG restrictions.[85]

---

[81] NSG plenary meeting, Aspen, Colo., 10–11 May 2001, Press statement, <http://www.sipri.org/contents/expcon/nsg_plenary01.html>.

[82] Joint Press Interaction of H. E. Shri Atal Bihari Vajpayee, Prime Minister of India and H.E. Mr. Vladimir Putin, President of the Russian Federation held at Hyderabad House, Ministry of External Affairs of India official website, 4 Dec. 2002, <http://meadev.nic.in/pbhome.htm>.

[83] Ministry of Foreign Affairs of the Russian Federation, 'On the plenary meeting of the Nuclear Suppliers Group' (unofficial translation from Russian), 28 May 2003, <http://www.mid.ru/brp_4.nsf/english>.

[84] Radyuhin, V., 'Russia for lifting ban on nuclear deals with India', The Hindu, 3 Nov. 2003, <http://www.hindu.com/2003/11/03/stories/2003110304141200.htm>.

[85] Siluyanova, P., 'Russia will float the "peaceful atom" to India', Gazeta, 13 Nov. 2003, <http://www.gzt.ru/business/2003/11/13/120700.html>; and Rumyantsev, A., [It is necessary

Sergei Kirienko, Alexander Rumyantsev's successor as the head of Russia's Federal Atomic Energy Agency[86], also called for lifting the NSG ban on nuclear trade with India. During his visit to India in April 2006 Kirienko stressed Russia's readiness to invest in India's nuclear energy industry, but only after restrictions are removed. Three major areas of cooperation were discussed between Russian and Indian officials during Kirienko's visit: first, the two Kudankulam reactors, currently scheduled for completion in 2007 and 2008; second, the possibility that, if and when NSG rules permit it, Russia could build at least four more reactors at the Kudankulam site; and third, the potential for cooperative development and construction of fast breeder reactors.[87]

Despite Russia's public statements, President Putin does not seem ready to recognize India as a nuclear weapon state. Putin has made a number of statements where he has clearly explained that he does not accept that there are new nuclear weapon states in the world, and that he does not think that Russia's acknowledgement of such states could lead to any positive results. Putin also stated that Russia would like India to sign the 1996 Comprehensive Nuclear Test-Ban Treaty (CTBT) and the NPT.[88]

The United States

In 2004 there was evidence of a change in thinking in the USA about the manner in which India's nuclear supply arrangements should be linked to IAEA safeguards. In June 2004 the Director of Policy Planning in the US State Department, Mitchell Reiss, said that the USA 'would like to see India place all its *civilian* facilities under IAEA safeguards'.[89]

Indian commentators were quick to point out that this was a change in the US position, which previously stressed the need for India to accept safeguards on its *entire* nuclear programme, civilian and mili-

to speed up the construction of the first reactor in Bushehr], *Vremya Novostey*, 17 Nov. 2003, <http://www.vremya.ru/print/85020.html> (in Russian).

[86] Minatom was reorganized in 2004 under the new title of the Federal Atomic Energy Agency (Rosatom).

[87] Kornysheva, A. and Shishkin, M., 'Sergei Kirienko offered India to build new reactors', *Kommersant*, 10 Apr. 2006.

[88] Fedchenko (note 65), p 69. The CTBT has not yet entered into force.

[89] Reiss, M., 'Power and responsibility: South Asia and world order', Keynote speech to the Conference on South Asia and the Nuclear Future, Stanford University, 4–5 June 2004, <http://cisac.stanford.edu/events/3889> (emphasis added).

tary.[90] A US proposal of the kind suggested by Reiss would, it was noted, ease cooperation with the Indian civilian nuclear sector without placing barriers in the way of the further development of India's nuclear deterrent. The differentiated approach to cooperation with the civil and military parts of the Indian nuclear establishment would mean treating India in a manner resembling nuclear weapon states as defined in the NPT.

In the days following the presentation by Reiss, unnamed US officials stressed that there was no immediate prospect of the sale of US nuclear reactors to India, something that 'would depend on a lot of steps being taken by both governments. It involves, among other things, taking steps to improve export controls, their legislation and implementation. We are not there yet. You cannot, however, exclude it as a possibility in the distant future'.[91]

This change in US Government thinking about nuclear supply to India was part of a wider re-evaluation of US–Indian relations by the Bush Administration. On 22 September 2001 President Bush issued Presidential Determination no. 2001–28, which lifted export control sanctions on India that were triggered after the 1998 Indian nuclear tests by the so-called 1994 Glenn Amendment.[92] This amendment prohibited all US economic and military assistance to any non-nuclear weapon state (as defined by the NPT) that conducted a nuclear test. In 2002 the USA began talks with India under the title of Next Steps in Strategic Partnership (NSSP). In 2002 the USA also began an active programme of dialogue with India on export control issues, including that of harmonizing Indian national controls with the NSG Guidelines. The NSSP talks led to agreement in January 2004 on a number of elements of expanded cooperation, one of which was to seek mutually beneficial economic opportunities in the civilian nuclear power sector.[93]

The contents of the NSSP programme were announced on 18 July 2005 in a joint statement by President Bush and Indian Prime Minister

---

[90] Chari, P. R., 'Indian N-facilities and IAEA safeguards: US demarche and Indian reality', *Deccan Herald*, 14 June 2004.

[91] 'US to boost N-ventures with India', *Indian Express*, 17 June 2004, <http://www. expressindia.com/fullstory.php?newsid=32656>.

[92] Nuclear Proliferation Prevention Act of 1994, 30 Apr. 1994, US Public Law 103-236.

[93] Rocca, C., Assistant Secretary for South Asian Affairs, 'The FY 2005 Foreign Assistance Budget Request for South Asia', Statement before the United States Senate Committee on Foreign Relations, 2 Mar. 2004.

Manmohan Singh.[94] The two leaders agreed that completion of the NSSP provides the basis for expanding bilateral activities and commerce in space, civil nuclear energy and dual-use technology. Each of the different technical areas of the NSSP programme has subsequently developed on parallel tracks, one of which is the Indian–US Civil Nuclear Cooperation Initiative (CNCI).[95]

President Bush has declared his view that 'as a responsible state with advanced nuclear technology, India should acquire the same benefits and advantages as other such states'. One part of the July 2005 joint statement elaborates actions that will be taken by the United States. Bush made commitments to 'work to achieve full civil nuclear energy cooperation with India', and accordingly to 'seek agreement from Congress to adjust US laws and policies, and . . . work with friends and allies to adjust international regimes to enable full civil nuclear energy cooperation and trade with India, including but not limited to expeditious consideration of fuel supplies for safeguarded nuclear reactors at Tarapur'.[96]

The Bush Administration also promised to consult with US partners on India's participation in the International Thermonuclear Experimental Reactor (ITER) consortium and support India's part in the work to develop advanced nuclear reactors.

In the joint statement India, for its part, pledged to 'reciprocally' agree to assume the same 'responsibilities and practices', and thereby acquire the same 'benefits and advantages', as other countries with advanced nuclear technology:

These responsibilities and practices consist of identifying and separating civilian and military nuclear facilities and programs in a phased manner and filing a declaration regarding its civilian nuclear facilities with the International Atomic Energy Agency (IAEA); taking a decision to place voluntarily its civilian nuclear facilities under IAEA safeguards; signing and adhering to an Additional Protocol with respect to civilian nuclear facilities; continuing India's unilateral moratorium on nuclear testing; working with the United States for the conclusion of a multilateral Fissile Material Cut Off Treaty; refraining from transfer of enrichment and reprocessing technologies to states that do not have them and supporting international efforts to limit their

---

[94] The White House, 'Joint statement between President George W. Bush and Prime Minister Manmohan Singh', Press release, Washington, DC, 18 July 2005, <http://www.whitehouse.gov/news/releases/2005/07/20050718-6.html>.

[95] Ahlström (note 59).

[96] The White House (note 94).

spread; and ensuring that the necessary steps have been taken to secure nuclear materials and technology through comprehensive export control legislation and through harmonization and adherence to Missile Technology Control Regime (MTCR) and Nuclear Suppliers Group (NSG) Guidelines.[97]

The USA and India formed a Joint Working Group on Civil Nuclear Energy Cooperation 'to undertake on a phased basis in the months ahead the necessary actions mentioned above to fulfill these commitments'. The US Under Secretary of State for Political Affairs, R. Nicholas Burns, underlined that 'for any agreement to be credible with the United States Congress and the Nuclear Suppliers Group, it's going to have to be a detailed agreement, it's going to have to be substantial'.[98] In January 2006 the Joint Working Group began to focus on preliminary ideas about the separation plan for civil and military facilities presented by India, as well as the kinds of safeguards that could be applied at the identified civilian facilities.

A specific separation plan was put forward by India prior to President Bush's visit to India in March 2006, opening the way for the launch of the CNCI at the summit meeting with Prime Minister Singh.[99] According to the separation plan, India would place an agreed set of existing civilian nuclear facilities as well as all future civilian nuclear facilities under safeguards agreed through permanent arrangements with the IAEA.[100] The agreement was said to include 65 per cent of India's total nuclear capacity. According to the Indian plan as described by US Under Secretary Burns, 'all future civilian thermal and breeder reactors will come under safeguards. So, as they add 1000-megawatt power plants, which we believe they will do in the near future, they will come under safeguards. And therefore, the percentage of increase, whether it's the number of reactors or megawattage under safeguards, is going to increase over time'.[101]

[97] The White House (note 94).

[98] Joint Press Interaction by Foreign Secretary Mr Shyam Saran and US Under Secretary of State Mr Nicholas Burns, New Delhi, 20 Jan. 2006, <http://mea.gov.in/pressbriefing/2006/01/20mi01.htm>.

[99] US Department of State, 'Bush, India's Singh sign civil nuclear cooperation agreement', 2 Mar. 2006, <http://usinfo.state.gov/sa/Archive/2006/Mar/02-806725.html>.

[100] Horner, D., 'US, India settle on separation plan for Indian civilian, nuclear weapons programs', *Nucleonics Week*, 9 Mar. 2006, pp. 1, 11–13.

[101] 'Bush admn. against renegotiating Indo-US nuke deal', Press Trust of India, 17 Mar. 2006.

In order for the CNCI to be implemented, the US Congress would first need to amend existing law in two ways. First, there are provisions in the 1978 Nuclear Non-Proliferation Act (NNPA) requiring non-nuclear weapon states as defined in the NPT to conclude full-scope safeguards with the IAEA before they can engage in peaceful nuclear cooperation with the USA.[102] India, which is not a party to the NPT, cannot meet this condition and the Congress would have to provide the US president with authority to waive certain conditions of that law if cooperation was to go ahead. Second, under the terms of the 1954 Atomic Energy Act (AEA) the USA requires a separate bilateral agreement with any country with which peaceful nuclear cooperation is envisaged.[103] This agreement is known as a '123 Agreement' because statutory authority to negotiate such an agreement stems from Section 123 of the AEA. The NNPA and the AEA also lay down the substantive conditions that must be contained in a bilateral agreement for peaceful nuclear cooperation. Since the 123 Agreement would need to be ratified by the US Congress, the Bush Administration opened a dialogue with the Congress on the provisions that would be included in the draft to be offered to India.

In March 2006 the Bush Administration submitted documents to the Congress laying out for its consideration the elements required to establish the legal provisions that would be necessary if the CNCI was to be implemented. The administration explained that the Congress would have to keep in mind the parameters already established in the existing agreement with India when evaluating amendments to US law. Under Secretary Burns stated that:

this is a complex agreement. To reopen it, we're probably at risk of never being able to achieve it again and to reassemble it. So what we've said to members of Congress who have raised this with us is that we welcome all ideas. There may be ideas that do not require renegotiation, that may help to reinforce or strengthen this agreement. We're open to all of them. But we wish not to renegotiate.[104]

---

[102] The 1978 Nuclear Non-Proliferation Act, 10 Mar. 1978, US Public Law 95-242, reproduced in *Nuclear Regulatory Legislation* (NUREG-0980), vol. 1, no. 6 (US Nuclear Regulatory Commission, Office of the General Counsel: Washington, DC, June 2002), pp. 151–53.

[103] The Atomic Energy Act of 1954, 30 Aug. 1954, US Public Law 83-703, reproduced in Nuclear Regulatory Legislation (note 102), pp. 52–56.

[104] 'Bush admn. against renegotiating Indo-US nuke deal' (note 101).

The CNCI raised some controversy in the USA.[105] The separation of India's nuclear activities into civilian and military components was one source of controversy. Under a separation plan the US and Indian governments have argued that India could demonstrate its commitment to preventing any support to nuclear weapon programmes of other states without jeopardizing its own nuclear weapon programme. India would be able to engage in international cooperation on the civilian part of its nuclear fuel cycle after implementing the most modern and effective non-proliferation controls. Meanwhile, because India's military programme would be sealed off from foreign cooperation, there would not be a proliferation risk from that quarter.

US officials pointed out that this broad approach was consistent with India's existing pattern of behaviour. US Under Secretary for Industry and Security Kenneth Juster, a senior official with responsibility for dual-use export control issues, has noted that India has a stake in the global non-proliferation regime and 'is working closely with the United States to stop proliferation'.[106] While the USA remains opposed to the Indian nuclear deterrent, the change in US policy is intended to create the basis for cooperation on shared objectives, such as economic development and reducing the risks of unauthorized access to sensitive and dangerous nuclear materials. The closer integration of India into the IAEA safeguards regime would open the door to Indian participation in other IAEA initiatives, including those related to nuclear safety and security. Meanwhile, a better understanding of Indian export controls and confidence that they meet recognized international standards would not only ease cooperation with the nuclear power industry, but also help to pinpoint actual or potential weaknesses in existing Indian laws, policies and practices that could then be addressed.

US critics of the CNCI raised technical, legal and political arguments against proceeding with deeper bilateral cooperation.[107] At a

---

[105] For one critical appraisal see the article by former Assistant Secretary of State for Non-proliferation Robert Einhorn, 'Limiting the damage', *National Interest*, vol. 82 (winter 2005–06), pp. 112–17.

[106] 'US dangles nuclear sop with control rider', *The Telegraph* (Calcutta), 21 Nov. 2003, <http://www.telegraphindia.com/1031121/asp/nation/story_2595213.asp>.

[107] Kimball, D., 'Civil, military separation plan not credible', *Asian Affairs*, Apr. 2006. The broader legal objections are discussed below and are described and analysed further in Ahlström (note 59), pp. 669–85. Technical objections related to foreign fuel access for India are discussed in Kile, S. N., 'Nuclear arms control and non-proliferation', *SIPRI Yearbook 2007* (note 25), pp. 495–97.

summit meeting in New Delhi on 2 March 2006, President Bush and Prime Minister Singh announced that they had reached agreement on how India could separate its nuclear programme into civilian and military components.[108] Some of the questions raised by the separation plan are directly pertinent to export control matters. They include both the question of how effective India's own export control system may be and how potential foreign partners could work with India's nuclear sector in the future while continuing to apply their own export controls.

Many individuals would have to change their status if the plan were implemented. Having previously worked in a nuclear sector where facilities and entities performed both a military and civilian function, they would in future find themselves in either the military or civilian sector. Further proliferation risks could be created if employees were later able to move across the boundary between sectors in either direction (i.e. from the military to the civil sector or vice versa). In the first case, barriers to transfer of so-called 'intangible technology' would be needed to prevent knowledge gained in the military programme from being shared outside India.[109] In the second case, barriers would be required to prevent relevant knowledge that Indian scientists and technicians acquired through international civilian nuclear cooperation from being applied in India's military programme.

Under the separation plan Indian officials emphasized that India retained the sole right to decide whether future facilities should be designated as civilian or military.[110] This would be a critical judgement from a non-proliferation perspective. The facilities included in the civilian sector would be subject to safeguards, and also far more likely to be engaged in international cooperation than facilities outside the safeguards system designated as elements of the military nuclear sector. Indian officials have underscored that the separation process should not in any way undermine the three-stage nuclear development plan created in the 1950s, which envisions a thorium-based closed

---

[108] The White House, 'President, Prime Minister Singh discuss growing strategic partnership', News release, New Delhi, 2 Mar. 2006, <http://www.whitehouse.gov/news/releases/2006/03/20060302-9.html>.

[109] Intangible technology is technical information transmitted orally (in face-to-face conversations or by telephone), visually (through participating in meetings or seminars) or electronically (in email or via wide area computer networks or the Internet).

[110] Indian Department of Atomic Energy, 'PM's Suo-Motu statement on discussions on civil nuclear energy cooperation with the US: implementation of India's separation plan', Press release, New Delhi, 7 Mar. 2006, <http://www.dae.gov.in/press/suopm0703.htm>.

fuel cycle.[111] This could mean that some of the facilities with which international partners are interested to cooperate would be held outside the safeguards system since India appears unwilling to place its fast breeder reactor programme (which is integral to the second stage of the development plan) under civilian safeguards.[112]

India has not published many details about the future status of other facilities vis-à-vis safeguards. As one general guideline the Indian Parliament was informed that facilities carrying out civilian activities but located in 'larger hubs of strategic significance' would not be designated as part of the civilian sector.[113] One Indian newspaper has reported that centres of nuclear research—the Bhabha Atomic Research Centre and the Indira Gandhi Centre for Atomic Research in Kalpakkam—are considered too sensitive to permit outside inspections of any of the facilities they contain, including facilities located at the sites that do not engage in military-related activities.[114] Similar arguments may apply to the Rattehalli uranium enrichment facilities located at Mysore and facilities on the site of the Nuclear Fuel Complex in Hyderabad.

The outcome of elections in the US Congress in November 2006 changed the balance between the Republican and Democratic parties in both the Senate and the House of Representatives at a time when legislative changes to facilitate the CNCI had not yet been agreed. In both the House of Representatives and the Senate the Democratic Party assumed control of key committees responsible for bringing legislation forward for approval. In the event the legislation was brought to a vote expeditiously in both houses of the Congress and approved by wide margins in each. President Bush signed the United States–India Peaceful Atomic Energy Cooperation Act into US law on 18 December 2006.[115]

---

[111] Indian Department of Atomic Energy (note 110).

[112] See Mian, Z. et al., 'Fissile materials in South Asia and the implications of the US–Indian nuclear deal', Draft report for the International Panel on Fissile Materials, 11 July 2006, <http://www.armscontrol.org/pdf/20060711_IPFM-DraftReport-US-India-Deal.pdf>.

[113] Embassy of India, Washington, DC, 'Implementation of India–United States joint statement of July 18, 2005: India's separation plan', Press release, 7 Mar. 2006, <http://www.indianembassy.org/newsite/press_release/2006/Mar/sepplan.pdf>.

[114] Varadarajan, S., 'Nuclear separation plan seeks fine balance', The Hindu, 8 Mar. 2006.

[115] The White House, 'President's statement on H.R. 5682, the "Henry J. Hyde United States–India Peaceful Atomic Energy Cooperation Act of 2006"', Press release, Washington, DC, 18 Dec. 2006, <http://www.whitehouse.gov/news/releases/2006/12/20061218-12.html>.

The legislative changes made in 2006 were one step in the overall process of implementing the CNCI because the new legal framework creates the conditions for negotiating the 123 Agreement that will establish a basis for peaceful nuclear cooperation between the USA and India. Once the 123 Agreement is negotiated and agreed between the executive authorities, the House of Representatives and the Senate will have to approve it before it can take effect, and it is likely that that the range of advantages and disadvantages of the CNCI will be debated once again in the United States.

France

France is another important nuclear supplier that has expressed an interest in cooperation with India for a number of years. When French President Jacques Chirac visited India in January 1998, a few months before the Indian nuclear tests, he stated that India could count on France to help meet its strategic needs and underlined that first and foremost it was power generation he had in mind. Chirac mentioned that, in the course of time, Indo-French energy cooperation could extend into the nuclear power field. However, while the initiative was strongly supported by India's President Kocheril Raman Narayanan, Chirac also made it clear that such cooperation was not yet possible.[116]

France did not change its political course as a result of the Indian nuclear tests. In June 1998 a delegation, including top officials from the Indian Department of Atomic Energy, made a visit to Paris for technical talks with French officials on both civilian nuclear cooperation and non-proliferation. The talks were described as a follow-up to the bilateral dialogue on aspects of civilian nuclear cooperation that was set in motion during Chirac's visit to India in January 1998. Press accounts interpreted the decision to proceed with the meeting as related to lobbying by the French nuclear power industry, said to have 'stepped up pressure on the government to find a way out of its international commitments and the political hurdles that come in the way of a deal with India'.[117]

In February 2000 French foreign minister Hubert Vedrine restated the desirability in principle of greater cooperation in the field of civilian nuclear technology but again stressed the obstacles. Vedrine

---

[116] Fedchenko, Shilin and Timerbaev (note 67), p. 20.

[117] George, N., 'Nuke deals: India now eyes France', *Indian Express*, 30 June 1998, <http://www.indianexpress.com/ie/daily/19980630/18150504.html>.

insisted that 'to be able to make progress in this field of cooperation, India has to show it is ready to go along with the international (nuclear) regimes'—a reference at that time to the need for India to sign the CTBT.[118] On 28 September 2002 the new foreign minister Dominique de Villepin repeated essentially the same position.[119] At the St Petersburg summit in June 2003 India's Prime Minister Atal Bihari Vajpayee raised the issue of the NSG Guidelines directly with President Chirac. Press reports at the time suggested that France was seeking a review of the NSG Guidelines.[120]

France's approach appears to have earned it a special position vis-à-vis India. India considers France and Russia to be states that will respond to pressure in order to change existing export control rules. If or when such a change takes place, France expects to have a privileged position as a nuclear supplier in the Indian market.[121]

III. Nuclear supplies to Iran: issues for the Nuclear Suppliers Group

While India has not joined the international non-proliferation regime, Iran is a party to the NPT and has accepted full-scope safeguards on its nuclear facilities. On 18 December 2003 Iran signed an Additional Protocol to its safeguards agreement with the IAEA. However, in spite of the fact that integrated safeguards will be in place for Iran, the issue of nuclear supply to the country has remained highly contentious for the NSG.

As noted in chapter 2, the NSG participating states should only authorize a transfer when satisfied that it will not contribute to the proliferation of nuclear weapons, meaning that factors such as adherence to the NPT do not by themselves guarantee a nuclear supply. The central issue for nuclear suppliers with regard to cooperation with Iran

---

[118] Mohan, C. R., 'Signing CTBT will help', *The Hindu*, 15 Feb. 2000.

[119] Interview given by Dominique de Villepin, French Minister of Foreign Affairs, to *The Hindu*, Paris, 28 Sep. 2002, <http://www.diplomatie.gouv.fr/actu/bulletin.gb.asp?liste=2002 1001.gb.html>.

[120] 'India: France, Russia want cooperation in "peaceful" uses of nuclear energy', *The Telegraph* (Calcutta), 1 June 2003.

[121] Malhotra, J., 'Rediscovering France', *Indian Express*, 18 Feb. 2000, <http://www.indianexpress.com/ie/daily/20000218/ian18046.html>; and Kozlov, V., [Perspectives of Russian atomic export], *Yaderny Kontrol*, no. 3, 69, vol. 9 (fall 2003), <http://www.pircenter.org/data/publications/yk3-2003.pdf>, p. 122. (in Russian).

is whether or not to invoke this principle, which in turn requires a judgement about Iranian compliance with the NPT.

Iranian observers have accepted the broad proposition that compliance with the NPT is the appropriate standard for nuclear suppliers to apply. However, Iran has argued that applying this standard should not be left to the sole discretion of nuclear suppliers. In April 1999 Cyrus Nasseri, an adviser to the Iranian Minister of Foreign Affairs stated that:

conditions to qualify for access are not arbitrary and left to individual decisions by State Parties. They are set by the Treaty. Those conditions, for the moment, are acceding to the NPT and accepting the FSS [full-scope safeguards]. Unless and until these conditions are modified by amending the NPT or Additional Protocols, they remain the sole conditions of eligibility. The only exception one might draw is when a member withdraws from the NPT or is proven, beyond a reasonable doubt, to be in flagrant violation of the NPT. In this very exceptional case, one could argue, that the State concerned has deprived itself of its own inalienable right until it stops its violations and decides again to comply. But evidence and proof that is clear and convincing is the minimum prerequisite.[122]

In the same presentation Nasseri criticized the subjective element in export licence assessment and asserted that 'the essential problem with the NSG is that it is viewed increasingly as a self-appointed body for NPT compliance. . . . Matters that it deals with relate to the core and essence of the NPT'.[123]

By increasing the amount and quality of information about the nuclear activities of states, the system of integrated safeguards that a growing number of countries (including Iran) are currently putting in place is likely to make it easier for governments to reach a political judgement about compliance with the NPT. In the past, however, the authorities responsible for making this judgement have had to base their decisions on a more limited range of information.

Under these circumstances the information exchanged within the NSG could be invaluable to export control authorities. This is likely to be particularly true in countries that do not have large or well-funded

---

[122] Nasseri, C., 'A prescription for evolution: the NSG's impact on non-proliferation and the right to access', Presentation to the 2nd NSG International Seminar on the Role of Export Controls in Nuclear Non-Proliferation, New York, N.Y., 8–9 Apr. 1999, p. 55.

[123] Nasseri (note 122), p. 56.

national intelligence services tasked with gathering the required information through national technical means.

The questions that authorities have been faced with have included the following: are the explanations offered by Iran about the end-use of nuclear items credible? Is the pattern of Iranian behaviour, particularly concerning the implementation of safeguards, consistent with statements about exclusively peaceful nuclear intentions? Is the pattern of Iranian acquisition of controlled materials, equipment and expertise consistent with statements about nuclear intentions and end-use?

The USA has long argued that Iran has sought materials, training, equipment and know-how from abroad to support a clandestine nuclear weapon programme. Iranian officials have insisted that the country's nuclear programme is intended solely to produce electricity and have emphasized that the development of nuclear energy for peaceful purposes is fully consistent with the terms of the NPT. However, US officials have dismissed arguments based on the need for Iran to develop additional sources of energy supply.[124]

In 2002 and 2003, evidence emerged that Iran had secretly pursued a range of nuclear fuel-cycle technologies, including enrichment and reprocessing, without declaring these activities to the IAEA (as required under the terms of its 1974 Safeguards Agreement with the agency).[125] This lack of transparency contributed to concerns that Iran might be putting into place, under the cover of a civil nuclear energy programme, the facilities needed to produce fissile material for a nuclear weapon.[126] Apart from transparency issues and doubts about the economic and developmental rationale for elements of the Iranian

[124] E.g. at the Preparatory Committee for the 2005 Review Conference of the NPT a US representative noted that 'Iran claims it is pursuing expensive and indigenous nuclear fuel-cycle facilities to meet expanding electricity demands, while preserving oil and gas for export. Such a rationale is very difficult to believe. In light of Iran's vast oil and gas reserves, the large expenditures it would make on nuclear facilities makes no economic or energy sense'. Semmel, A. K., Deputy Assistant Secretary, US Department of State, 'Regional non-proliferation issues: Remarks to the second session of the preparatory committee for the 2005 NPT Review Conference', Geneva, 2 May 2003, <http://www.state.gov/t/np/rls/rm/ 20283. htm>.

[125] IAEA Board of Governors, 'Implementation of the NPT safeguards agreement in the Islamic Republic of Iran', GOV/2003/40, 6 June 2003, <http://www.iaea.org/Publications/Documents/Board/2003/gov2003-40.pdf>.

[126] The background to Iran's IAEA safeguards programme, including recent disputes and developments, is discussed in Kile, S. N. (ed.), *Europe and Iran: Perspectives on Non-proliferation*, SIPRI Research Report no. 21 (Oxford University Press: Oxford, 2005).

nuclear programme, Iran's pattern of acquisition of dual-use items has also been pointed to as an additional indicator of Iranian intentions.

Russia, an important cooperation partner of Iran, has rejected the US argument that the supply of nuclear material to Iran is inconsistent with the non-proliferation principle regardless of Iran's adherence to the NPT and Tehran's decision to put in place integrated IAEA safeguards. One major foreign contribution to the Iranian nuclear programme is the construction of the nuclear power plant near the town of Bushehr in south-eastern Iran. In the early 1970s Shah Mohammad Reza Pahlavi decided that Iran's energy sources needed to be diversified and nuclear energy was chosen as one alternative. In 1974 the Shah established the Atomic Energy Organization of Iran (AEOI) and approved a nuclear energy programme based on developing the full nuclear fuel cycle inside the country.[127]

At that time, France, Germany and the USA were chosen as the main potential nuclear suppliers. Iran also conducted negotiations with, among others, Belgium, China, India, Italy, Switzerland and the UK. In 1974 the AEOI signed an agreement with the German firm Kraftwerk Union to build two 1200 megawatt-electric (MW(e)) pressurized water reactors near Bushehr, and with the French firm Framatome to install two 930 MW(e) reactors at Darkhovin, near the city of Ahvaz, in south-western Iran. In 1975 Iran signed an agreement with the USA for the purchase of eight reactors. The US Atomic Energy Commission then agreed to supply Iran with fuel for two 1200 MW(e) light-water reactors and signed a provisional agreement to supply fuel for up to six additional reactors with a total power capacity of 8000 MW(e).[128] In the framework of its overall nuclear programme, Iran also explored cooperation with a number of potential suppliers of uranium enrichment and plutonium reprocessing facilities.[129]

When the Islamic revolution took place in Iran in 1978–79 few of the activities in these agreements had commenced. Iran had one small operational research reactor in Tehran (supplied by the USA) and two unfinished power reactors in Bushehr. One of the reactors in Bushehr was reported to be 75–85 per cent complete at the time of the revo-

---

[127] Khlopkov, A., *Iran's Nuclear Program in Russian–American Relations*, PIR Study Paper no. 18 (PIR Center: Moscow, 2001), <http://www.pircenter.org/data/publications/nz18.pdf>, pp. 5, 7

[128] Nuclear Threat Initiative, 'Iran profile: nuclear chronology', <http://www.nti.org/e_research/profiles/Iran/1825.html>.

[129] Nuclear Threat Initiative (note 128).

lution, and the other 45–70 per cent complete.[130] After the revolution, nuclear suppliers halted all nuclear cooperation activities. Kraftwerk Union and Framatome withdrew from the nuclear power projects, and contacts with the USA were discontinued. Moreover, during the 1980–88 Iran–Iraq War, Iraq attacked the Bushehr site and the reactors were damaged. Iran's subsequent attempts to revive the Bushehr project encountered difficulties in conditions where preventing Iran from obtaining nuclear technologies that might contribute to weapon programmes had become a major US concern. During the early 1990s Iran tried but failed to establish nuclear cooperation with Argentina, Belgium, Brazil, Germany, India and Spain.

China and Iran signed a framework agreement for the construction of nuclear facilities in 1985 and subsequently held a number of discussions to translate the agreement into a more specific undertaking on equipment supply.[131] In 1992 an agreement to supply two Chinese reactors to Iran led to the award of contracts for the project in 1994.[132] However, China had mostly discontinued its nuclear cooperation with Iran by 1997, largely because of pressure from the USA, which linked progress in Sino-US nuclear cooperation to the discontinuation of all but two projects between China and Iran.[133] In 1995 Russia stepped in to assist Iran with the Bushehr project.[134]

Russian nuclear assistance

Iranian–Russian nuclear cooperation dates back to 1987–88, when discussions began between high-ranking officials. Peaceful nuclear cooperation with Iran is part of a broader long-term commercial, economic, scientific and technical cooperation between Iran and the

[130] Perabo, B., 'A chronology of Iran's nuclear program', *Eye on Supply*, no. 7 (Sep. 1992), pp. 45–71.

[131] Hibbs, M., Patri, N. and Sandler, N., 'US, Europe doubt Israeli claim of Iranian nuclear weapons effort', *Nuclear Fuel*, no. 24, vol. 16 (25 Nov. 1991), p. 8.

[132] Konstantin, M., 'Russia, PRC, links to Iranian nuclear program assessed', *Al-Majallah* (London), 17 Dec. 1995, pp. 50–54, in Foreign Broadcast Information Service, *Daily Report– Arms Control (FBIS-TAC)*, FBIS-TAC-96-004, 22 Mar. 1996. China also agreed to supply a facility to Iran to manufacture cladding for nuclear fuel and equipment for a uranium conversion facility to produce uranium hexafluoride.

[133] Koch, A. and Wolf, J., *Iran's Nuclear Facilities: A Profile* (Center for Nonproliferation Studies, Monterey Institute for International Studies: Monterey, Calif., 1998), <http://cns.miis.edu/pubs/reports/pdfs/iranrpt.pdf>.

[134] Fedchenko, V., Fedorov, R. and Mamedova, N., 'Iran's nuclear program and Russian– Iranian relations', Institute for Applied International Research, Policy Paper no. 2, (Feb. 2003).

former USSR signed on 22 June 1989.[135] In August 1992 Iran and Russia signed two agreements: On Building a Nuclear Power Plant and On Cooperation in Peaceful Uses of Nuclear Energy. Under the first agreement, Iran wanted a nuclear power plant to be built in northern Iran, but geological analysis showed that the risk of seismic activity in the area was too high. Therefore it was decided in 1995 to continue the work at the Bushehr site instead. Under the second agreement, Russia agreed, in particular, to train Iranian specialists and to build a research reactor in Iran.[136]

In January 1995 Russian Atomic Energy Minister Victor Mikhailov signed an $800 million contract with Reza Amrollahi, head of the AEOI, committing Russia to complete one 1000 MW(e) reactor at Bushehr. In the protocol to this agreement Minatom agreed to supply Iran with various facilities, including light-water research reactors, fuel fabrication facilities and a uranium enrichment centrifuge plant.

Protests at the highest level by US President Bill Clinton to Russian President Boris Yeltsin led Russia to promise to cancel aspects of the agreement that could help Iran militarily. In December 1995 Russian Prime Minister Victor Chernomyrdin sent a confidential letter to US Vice-President Al Gore stating that Russia would limit its cooperation with Iran to Unit 1 of the Bushehr plant and the supply of the related fuel and training. The commitment was to cover a five-year period.[137]

The issue of Iranian–Russian nuclear cooperation re-emerged as a problem in Russian–US relations with the appointment of a new Russian Minister for Nuclear Energy, Evgeny Adamov, in March 1998. Adamov openly advocated selling additional power and research reactors to Iran and, as soon as he took office, Iranian–Russian nuclear cooperation at the level of research institutes increased. By the autumn of 1999 construction of the reactor building at Bushehr was virtually complete and the reactor equipment was purchased. Approximately 300 Russian enterprises (employing close to 20 000 people) participated in producing this equipment.[138]

[135] Ivanov, A. and Perera, J., 'Russian–Iranian nuclear cooperation', 25 June 1998, <http://www.oneworld.org/ips2/june98/18_19_076.html>.

[136] Mikhaylov, V., 'Minatom and international cooperation', *Yaderny Kontrol*, vol. 44, no. 2 (Mar./Apr. 1999), <http://www.pircenter.org/data/publications/yk2-1999.pdf>, pp. 62–66.

[137] Einhorn, R. and Samore, G., 'Ending Russian assistance to Iran's nuclear bomb', *Survival*, vol. 44 (summer 2002), p. 53.

[138] Khlopkov (note 127), p. 14.

When President Putin replaced Adamov with Alexander Rumyantsev in March 2001, US concerns about possible additional Russian sales abated somewhat. The supply of more sensitive fuel-cycle
facilities to Iran is no longer discussed seriously in Russia and,
although the press often mentions the possible supply of new nuclear
power plants to Iran, the prospects for such transactions seem quite
remote. The Iranian request to purchase more reactors dates from
1996 and has been repeated periodically ever since, including during
meetings at the level of heads of state and government.[139] However,
the prospect for any new nuclear reactor export to Iran has been
greatly reduced by the deterioration in relations between Iran and the
IAEA, discussed below.

Russia has also acted responsibly as regards the most sensitive issue
of the Bushehr project—nuclear fuel supplies. Russian officials made
clear from the very beginning that Iran must return nuclear fuel to
Russia after irradiation in the reactor and made construction of the
reactors conditional on this point. Iran and Russia needed to sign a
supplementary agreement on the return of spent nuclear fuel because
the issue was not fully formalized in the original reactor construction
contract. (This was largely because at around the same time Russian
legislators passed a package of laws that banned nuclear waste
imports.) In July 2001 Russia passed a new law that allowed imports
of spent nuclear fuel, enabling an Iranian–Russian agreement on spent
fuel to be reached and subsequent governmental regulations.[140]

Minatom drafted the elements of this agreement in the summer of
2002 and Iran accepted the general principle.[141] However, the Iranian
Government questioned the customary practice by which the state that
provides and takes back the nuclear fuel is paid for its storage and
reprocessing. Iran claimed that spent nuclear fuel is a valuable asset
and therefore Iran should be compensated for returning it. Negotiations to reconcile the Iranian and Russian positions on this issue took

---

[139] Mikhaylov (note 136).

[140] Manushkin, A., 'Pod kontrolem kazhdiy atom' [Every atom is under control], Kras-
naya Zvezda, 21 Aug. 2002, <http://www.redstar.ru/2002/08/21_08/1_02.html>. The package
included laws On Special Environmental Programs for the Rehabilitation of Radiation-
Contaminated Regions of the Territory; On the Insertion of Additions to the law On the Use
of Atomic Energy; and On the Insertion of Additions to Article 50 of the Russian Federation
Law on Environmental Protection. The texts of these laws are available at <http://www.
nti.org/db/nisprofs/russia/legslat/legislat.htm#7102001>.

[141] 'Iran–Russia: ministers formalize spent-fuel agreement', Global Security Newswire,
22 Aug. 2002, <http://www.nti.org/d_newswire/issues/2002/8/22/3s.html>.

a long time: the agreement on the nuclear fuel for Bushehr was signed only in February 2005.[142] Some experts have asserted that the need to work out procedures for temporary storage of spent nuclear fuel in Iran may also have been a cause of delay.[143] Spent fuel would normally be stored for three years in a special facility after being unloaded from a reactor prior to transportation. In the case of Iran, discussions were reportedly underway to reduce this period because of US pressure to remove the fuel from Iran as quickly as possible.

The IAEA and Iran

The system of IAEA safeguards does not verify compliance with the NPT. Any assessment of compliance requires that individual countries make their own judgement. The development of integrated safeguards has increased the degree of transparency regarding the nuclear activities of many states and this, taken together with the operational elements of safeguards such as regular reporting and inspection, can be a great aid to states when assessing compliance.[144]

Iran joined the IAEA in 1958 and signed the NPT in 1970. Iran also signed the CTBT in 1996. On signing the NPT, Iran assumed the obligation not to obtain, from any source whatsoever, nuclear explosive devices. Iran negotiated a safeguards agreement with the IAEA that entered into force on 15 May 1974. Under that agreement the IAEA has the right and responsibility to control any significant quantities of nuclear materials declared to exist in Iran. Iran must provide the IAEA with information on the facilities where such materials are either produced or in use. However, the 1974 safeguards agreement only allows IAEA inspectors to visit facilities that Iran has declared to the agency as being places where nuclear material of the kind subject to safeguards is located.

Safeguards agreements entail the submission to the IAEA of so-called subsidiary arrangements: documents containing technical infor-

---

[142] 'Russia and Iran signed the agreement on the return of the spent fuel', *RIA Novosti*, 27 Feb. 2006, <http://www.rian.ru/economy/20050227/39465595.html>.

[143] Khlopkov, A. and Lata, V., 'Iran's missile and nuclear challenge', *Yaderny Kontrol*, vol. 9, no. 2 (summer 2003), <http://www.pircenter.org/data/publications/yk2-2003.pdf>, p. 52.

[144] For a full assessment of the relationship between safeguards, transparency and verification see Maerli, M. B. and Johnston, R. G., 'Safeguarding this and verifying that: fuzzy concepts, confusing terminology, and their detrimental effect on nuclear husbandry', *Nonproliferation Review*, no. 1, vol. 2 (spring 2002), <http://www.cns.miis.edu/pubs/npr/search.htm>.

mation relevant to the nuclear materials and fuel-cycle facilities that were declared to the agency in the agreement. Subsidiary arrangements are necessary if the IAEA is to effectively implement a safeguards agreement.

Safeguards agreements were only designed to provide the IAEA with information concerning the nuclear material subject to safeguards and the features of facilities relevant to safeguarding that material. The subsidiary arrangements with Iran in force after 1976 required it to declare a given nuclear facility (and to provide design information on it) no later than 180 days before the introduction of nuclear material to this facility.

At the end of 2002 commercial satellite images were published on the Internet showing the construction of two nuclear fuel facilities south of Tehran.[145] Analysis by the non-governmental group that published the images determined that one of the facilities, near the town of Natanz, was a uranium enrichment plant; the other facility, near the town of Arak, appeared to be intended for the production of heavy water. Heavy water is an essential element in enabling a natural uranium reactor to produce plutonium that is suitable for use in nuclear weapons.

The discovery of the previously undeclared facilities was alarming from a proliferation perspective, since it suggested that Iran was covertly pursuing two alternative routes—uranium enrichment and plutonium separation—to obtain weapon-grade fissile material. However, when the nuclear facilities under construction in Iran were discovered, there was no legitimate basis for the IAEA to insist on visiting these facilities because they were undeclared.[146] The IAEA acted quickly and managed to persuade Iran to accept modifications to its subsidiary arrangements along the lines of a proposal made by the IAEA Board of Governors in 1992. The Board of Governors had requested the early provision of design information on new facilities and on modifications to existing facilities. In February 2003 the Iranian Government

[145] Albright, D. and Hinderstein, C., 'Iran building nuclear fuel cycle facilities: international transparency needed', Institute for Science and International Security (ISIS), ISIS Issues Brief, 12 Dec. 2002, <http://www.isis-online.org/publications/iran/iranimages.html>.

[146] Albright and Hinderstein (note 145).

confirmed its acceptance of the change to the subsidiary arrangements in a letter to the IAEA.[147]

The IAEA and the international community managed to persuade Iran to sign an Additional Protocol on 18 December 2003 and to submit its expanded declaration associated with the protocol on 22 May 2004.[148] Although Iran did not ratify the Additional Protocol using its national procedures, officials stated that they were acting in accordance with its provisions, pending formal entry into force.[149]

At the same time, during its investigations the IAEA continued to find serious problems with the implementation of safeguards in Iran. The IAEA Board of Governors, in its resolution of 18 June 2004, underlined that although the agency was making progress in gaining a comprehensive understanding of Iran's nuclear programme, a number of questions remained, including issues considered to be 'key to understanding the extent and nature of Iran's enrichment programme: the sources of all HEU contamination in Iran and the extent and nature of work undertaken using the P-2 advanced centrifuge design'.[150]

The concerns expressed by IAEA Director General Mohammed ElBaradei in March 2006 remain the prevailing view: namely that after 'years of intensive verification, there remain uncertainties with regard to both the scope and the nature of Iran's nuclear programme' and that the continued uncertainty was 'a matter of concern that continues to give rise to questions about the past and current direction of Iran's nuclear programme'.[151]

In addition to remaining questions from the past, at the beginning of 2006 Iran resumed certain nuclear activities that it had voluntarily suspended in 2003 during discussions with France, Germany and the UK. On 3 January 2006 Iran informed the IAEA that as of 10 January 2006 it would resume research and development associated with the

[147] IAEA, 'Introductory statement by IAEA Director General Mohamed ElBaradei to the Board of Governors', Vienna, 17 Mar. 2003, <http://www.iaea.org/NewsCenter/Statements/2003/ebsp2003n008.shtml>.

[148] IAEA, 'Iran signs Additional Protocol on nuclear safeguards', 18 Dec. 2003, <http://www.iaea.org/NewsCenter/News/2003/iranap20031218.html>.

[149] IAEA (note 148).

[150] IAEA Board of Governors, 'Implementation of the NPT safeguards agreement in the Islamic Republic of Iran', GOV/2004/49, 18 June 2004, <http://www.iaea.org/Publications/Documents/Board/2004/gov2004-49.pdf>.

[151] IAEA, 'Introductory statement to the Board of Governors by IAEA Director General Dr. Mohamed ElBaradei', Vienna, 6 Mar. 2006, <http://www.iaea.org/NewsCenter/Focus/IaeaIran/index.shtml>.

enrichment of uranium.[152] Iran stressed that it would conduct these activities in accordance with its safeguards agreement with the IAEA and that the activities were not planned for nuclear fuel production. However, in January 2006 Iran announced that it would no longer act in accordance with the Additional Protocol to its safeguards agreement, which it claimed it had been doing on a voluntary basis since December 2003.

The resumption of these activities has created additional uncertainties around the Iranian nuclear programme, which export licensing authorities could take into account when considering how to apply the NSG Guidelines—in particular the non-proliferation principle.

Iranian procurement activities

Monitoring and analysing the procurement activities of states can also provide evidence that can be applied in evaluating nuclear intentions and compliance. If a number of components are identified that, taken together, represent a coherent and disturbing pattern, authorities may question a country's overall intentions with regard to nuclear (or for that matter biological or chemical) weapons.

One component is the building up of general competence in the nuclear area. When this competence is being developed in organizations under the control of the military or in a new authority that is isolated from the wider national research and technology base, there may be cause for concern. A sudden, large increase in resources devoted to the development of this technical competence might also be taken as an important indicator of intentions, as could the establishment of closer ties with the research and development base in countries that are themselves a cause for concern.

Reducing vulnerabilities arising from dependence on foreign supply is likely to be a second component within the overall acquisition strategy of a state seeking nuclear weapons. Therefore, acquisition activities may target equipment and technology that will provide the national authorities with access to the elements of a weapon programme from domestic sources. This possibility is what lies at the

---

[152] Statement by Ambassador A. A. Soltanieh, Resident Representative of the Islamic Republic of Iran to the IAEA, Vienna, 2 Feb. 2006, <http://www.iaea.org/NewsCenter/Focus/IaeaIran/index.shtml>.

root of the international concern about civil nuclear power pro-grammes and nuclear research activities.

A third component of a wider acquisition strategy is likely to be a systematic and dedicated effort to collect public information that could be relevant to a weapon programme. This could include the use of trade or academic exchanges to gather information and, increas-ingly, the use of the Internet and other wide-area electronic networks as an information resource. The participation of intelligence officers and agencies in delegations of different kinds, and commercial con-tacts made by identifiable 'front' companies seeking technical infor-mation and specifications, are likely to raise concerns. An obvious example would be a new or previously unknown company (in par-ticular a small, perhaps one-person, firm) taking a close interest in the characteristics of controlled items. Concerns will naturally be higher if these contacts are made with one of the few sources of the most advanced technologies or materials that are particularly critical to a weapon programme.

A fourth component in the overall acquisition programme is the attempt to develop capacities that will later be required for testing and then fielding a nuclear weapon, including delivery systems. This would include acquiring skills for personnel to operate the system as well as competence and equipment needed for diagnostics and testing.

Many activities that might be carried out in any one of these areas would not be significant in isolation. However, taken together, such activities could be a cause for concern. Some analysts, including both governmental and non-governmental specialists, have concluded that Iranian activities have taken place in most if not all of the areas that suggest an illicit procurement strategy.

Discussing Iranian acquisition of dual-use items, David Albright observed that 'US and European intelligence agencies have collected considerable information about suspicious procurement efforts in Europe and elsewhere that suggest military intentions. Western intelli-gence officials have closely followed reports that Iranian agents have travelled throughout the former Soviet Union in search of nuclear materials, "know-how," and scientists.'[153] In a report published in 2003 by the Swedish Security Police, it was noted that 'as concerns the development of nuclear weapons, there are many indications that

---

[153] Albright, D., 'An Iranian bomb?', *Bulletin of the Atomic Scientists*, vol. 51, no. 5, (July/Aug. 1995), <http://www.thebulletin.org/issues/1995/ja95/ja95toc.html>.

Iran, Libya, North Korea and possibly Algeria, more or less actively, are engaged in a procurement process'. The report later notes that 'the actors that are engaged in a continuous and systematic effort to acquire dual-use products in Sweden are Iran, North Korea, Pakistan, Russia and India'.[154]

In 2003 the international dimension of Iranian procurement activities became a central focus when information that Iran provided to the IAEA suggested that Iran had acquired centrifuges used for uranium enrichment from Pakistan.[155] Subsequently, Iranian officials stated that at least five middlemen had facilitated access to equipment and technologies acquired from suppliers in different countries, including Germany, the Netherlands, South Africa and Sri Lanka.[156]

In the same year, French authorities raised questions about another aspect of Iranian nuclear procurement—efforts to purchase items that could be used in reprocessing nuclear fuel to extract plutonium. At the NSG plenary meeting in May 2003 in Busan, South Korea, France presented a paper on aspects of the Iranian nuclear programme. The paper noted the confirmation that a large heavy water production plant was being constructed (and was near completion) at Arak in Iran.[157] This facility would be capable of producing approximately 100 tonnes of heavy water each year. In June 2003 the IAEA confirmed that Iran was also planning to build a heavy water research reactor on the site at Arak.[158] In July Iran explained to IAEA inspectors that it needed a heavy water moderated reactor to produce radioactive isotopes for research purposes. Iran also described the design of the facility.

In August 2003 the IAEA was provided with supplementary information but noted that this did not contain any references to hot cells, which it described as 'contrary to what would be expected' given the

---

[154] Swedish Security Police, 'The proliferation of weapons of mass destruction', May 2003, <http://www.securityservice.se>, pp. 8, 9.

[155] IAEA Board of Governors, 'Implementation of the NPT Safeguards Agreement in the Islamic Republic of Iran', GOV/2003/75, 10 Nov. 2003, <http://www.iaea.org/Publications/Documents/Board/2003/gov2003-75.pdf>, p 4.

[156] Rohde, D., 'Pakistan questions 8 linked to nuclear program', New York Times, 19 Jan. 2004, <http://www.nytimes.com/2004/01/19/international/asia/19STAN.html>.

[157] 'Latest developments in the nuclear program of Iran, in particular on the plutonium way', Presentation by France at the NSG Information Exchange Meeting, Busan, South Korea 22–23 May 2003.

[158] IAEA Board of Governors, 'Implementation of the NPT safeguards agreement of the Islamic Republic of Iran,' GOV/2003/40, 6 June 2003, <http://www.iaea.org/Publications/Documents/Board/2003/gov2003-40.pdf>, p. 6.

declared purpose of the reactor.[159] Moreover, in its presentation to the 2003 NSG plenary, France questioned the quantity of heavy water to be produced at the facility in Arak, noting that it was far in excess of what Iran would need for civilian applications. French representatives reported attempts by Iran at the end of 2000 to buy 10 high-density shielding windows of a type suitable for use in a hot cell or reprocessing facility. France also reported that in 2002 an end-user in the United Arab Emirates tried to buy 28 remote manipulators that were above the NSG threshold for control and suitable for use in the environment likely to be found in a hot cell.

French concerns about Iranian procurement have not been allayed, and in February 2006 French Minister for Foreign Affairs Philippe Douste-Blazy stated that 'no civilian nuclear programme can explain the Iranian nuclear programme. It is a clandestine military nuclear programme'.[160]

The impact of Iranian activities on nuclear export licensing

The national export control authorities of NSG participating states need to take their decisions in the light of technical assessments about the potential end-use of the items being exported. However, they also need to take into account broader considerations related to Iranian nuclear activities in the context of obligations contained in the NPT, including those related to accepting IAEA safeguards.

The existing NSG Guidelines include a non-proliferation principle that requires authorities to take this broad approach to assessment. However, this principle is not accompanied by more specific criteria that would help participating states to be confident that they are applying it in a common and uniform manner. In fact, the approach to nuclear cooperation with Iran in the past underlines that there has not been a uniform standard for the application of the principle. There is no common understanding among states about whether or not Iran is fully compliant with the NPT. However, even in cases in which NSG participating states could agree on the status of Iranian compliance, there could still be divergent approaches to export licence assessment.

---

[159] IAEA Board of Governors (note 155), pp. 8–9. A 'hot cell' is a room that is protected in ways that permit manipulation of highly radioactive materials.

[160] 'France: Iran program "military"', CNN, 16 Feb. 2006, <http://www.cnn.com/2006/WORLD/meast/02/16/iran.france/index.html>.

These divergences might be caused by different interpretations of the non-proliferation principle. For example, in cases where countries felt able to authorize supply it might be on the technical grounds that the particular items concerned were peripheral to any possible military nuclear activities. It might also be that the particular nuclear supplier was satisfied with assurances that the items supplied would not be used for proscribed purposes, even though the technical characteristics of such items would be of potential use in a military programme.

4. Meeting the challenges facing the Nuclear Suppliers Group

I. Introduction

In chapters 1–3 it is shown that a growing number of states have accepted the need for effective national export controls. Although these states have taken steps to establish and implement controls, a number of questions have been raised about whether these controls are achieving their objective of blocking proliferation. In the light of these debates, the NSG has been engaged in discussions about what kinds of measure could increase the effectiveness of nuclear export controls.

The NSG requires consensus in its decision making about revisions to its guidelines. The progressive expansion in the number of NSG participants without any change in the rules for decision making has complicated the process of reaching agreement. Expanded participation has created a group that has diverse export control traditions and relatively little shared experience when compared to, for example, the cooperation carried out during the cold war in the framework of the Coordinating Committee for Multilateral Export Controls (COCOM).

The preferred approach of the NSG has been to develop guidelines for use by the national authorities of participating states when assessing applications to export listed items. Each national export control authority makes an independent interpretation of these guidelines without direct consultation with NSG partners when assessing such applications. This approach has given nuclear export control officials in different countries a degree of flexibility and discretion because individual applications can be judged against the guidelines and in the light of available information. However, if different national authorities interpret the guidelines in a manner that is too diverse there is a risk that the overall effectiveness of the control system will be compromised.

Some observers have questioned the manner in which states apply the NSG Guidelines at the national level. Chapter 3 notes that some Russian exports—actual or proposed—to India have raised questions from NSG partners. However, some analysts have identified a general problem with the implementation of export controls by Russia. In 2002 Leonard Spector wrote that Russia, 'driven by the desire for profit, is engaged in a wide range of unwise exports. The Bush Administration has highlighted Russia's disturbing trade with Iran in the nuclear and missile areas, which I will not reiterate here. But the Russian government is also permitting—indeed encouraging—other, highly disturbing exports'.[161] To support his assertion, Spector cited Russian nuclear exports and nuclear cooperation with India, Libya, Myanmar (Burma) and Syria.

One way to address this problem of diverse interpretation could be to introduce additional guidelines for general application that have an objective basis. A number of ideas for such guidelines have been put forward and these are examined in section II of this chapter.

The NSG may have reached a point where the general guidelines for global application need to be supplemented by country-specific rules for exports to destinations of concern. This would prevent participating states from taking divergent approaches to these destinations, which could undermine the cohesion and effectiveness of the export control system as a whole. The idea of adopting country-specific guidelines for nuclear transfers is examined in section III.

A third set of challenges relates to the issue of whether the NSG has the right set of participating states to tackle current and future proliferation challenges.

As noted above, from one point of view it can be argued that the NSG has already grown too large to be consistent in applying its existing rules. However, there is no procedure for expelling countries from the NSG and that option is not considered here.

The NSG does not contain all of the countries that have nuclear industries or industrial capacities that would be highly relevant from a non-proliferation perspective. Moreover, in the coming years the group of states that either have or seek such industries and industrial capacities may grow larger, given the interest expressed by a number of states—as noted in the first chapter of this report—in expanding nuclear power as an element of energy strategy. From this angle, the number of participating states in the NSG could be seen as too small.

---

[161] Spector, L. S., Deputy Director, Monterey Institute of International Studies, Center for Nonproliferation Studies, 'Russian exports of sensitive equipment and technology', Testimony before the Subcommittee on International Security, Proliferation, and Federal Services of the US Senate Committee on Governmental Affairs, 6 June 2002, <http://cns.miis.edu/pubs/reports/testspec.htm>. For a similar analysis from the same congressional hearing see Albright, D., Institute for Science and International Security, 'Nuclear non-proliferation concerns and export controls in Russia', <http://www.isis-online.org/testimony.html>.

One broad change aimed partly at addressing the difficulty of 'right sizing' nuclear export control cooperation has been prompted by Mohamed ElBaradei in a proposal that export controls should be carried out in a truly international framework, including a change in the legal form of cooperation. In February 2004 ElBaradei proposed the establishment of 'binding, treaty-based controls'.[162] In April 2004 the UN adopted Security Council Resolution 1540, which includes an instruction to states to put in place effective export controls. The resolution is binding on all UN member states and therefore has the characteristics of a clear legal basis for global participation sought by ElBaradei. Section IV evaluates the emerging global framework for nuclear supply.

A fourth set of challenges relates to the enforcement of agreed controls. If participating states were to conclude that inappropriate nuclear transfers take place because of lax enforcement by partners—in effect tolerating transfers that are inconsistent with the agreed guidelines (rather than different interpretations of the guidelines)—this would seriously degrade the effectiveness of the NSG. Evidence that national enforcement was being strengthened would be a valuable confidence-building measure within the NSG. This is considered in section V.

The NSG collects and shares information about the activities of intermediaries and front companies in order to strengthen enforcement. National export control authorities could work more closely with colleagues that share the commitment to non-proliferation and that have complementary capacities: for example, with the IAEA, which collects information in the context of implementing nuclear safeguards as well as gathering and storing information about illicit trafficking events. The Proliferation Security Initiative (PSI) was established in 2003 with the objective of disrupting the procurement networks used by countries of proliferation concern.[163] There may be scope for fruitful cooperation between the NSG, the IAEA and the PSI to strengthen enforcement of nuclear export controls. However, the representatives of some participants in the multilateral arms control

---

[162] ElBaradei (note 1).

[163] On behalf of the participating states, Canada has stated that the PSI aims 'to impede and stop illegal shipments of weapons of mass destruction (WMD), their delivery systems and related materials'. See the PSI website at <http://www.proliferationsecurity.info/introduction. html>. See also Ahlström, C., 'The Proliferation Security Initiative: international law aspects of the Statement of Interdiction Principles', *SIPRI Yearbook 2005* (note 13), pp. 741–65.

community regard the question of close ties and information sharing between the IAEA—which is open to all states that wish to join—and the NSG as highly sensitive. As discussed below, this cooperation will probably have to be managed through exchanging information among states that are represented on the IAEA Board of Governors or the special committee established by the IAEA to strengthen safeguards.

II. Strengthening nuclear export control guidelines

Guidelines that narrow the range of circumstances in which national authorities could authorize exports of nuclear or nuclear-related dual-use items might restore a common interpretation and common purpose to nuclear export controls. This might include adopting new conditions of supply.

In a speech delivered to the US National Defense University on 11 February 2004 President Bush outlined two suggestions to strengthen the NSG Guidelines.[164] The first was that an Additional Protocol to the bilateral safeguards agreement between a state and the IAEA should be a condition for the transfer of nuclear controlled items to that state. The second suggestion was to deny the transfer of items associated with the most sensitive parts of the nuclear fuel cycle (uranium enrichment and spent-fuel reprocessing) to states that do not already have such capacities.

The Additional Protocol as a condition of supply

In considering adapted guidelines, one main task for the NSG should be to revisit the question of what kinds of activity can be considered to be 'in conformity' with the NPT in the light of the information that has emerged recently about the procurement activities of states that are parties to that treaty. If it has been demonstrated that the level of assurance provided by a full-scope safeguards agreement with the IAEA is insufficient to identify a legitimate end-use and a legitimate end-user, what supplemental measures might be adequate to provide that assurance? The strengthening of the IAEA safeguards system provides a clear and objective point of reference for a modern understanding of what compliance with the NPT should mean.

---

[164] The White House (note 14).

The motive forces behind the IAEA's 1997 decision to approve the Additional Protocol as a potential condition of supply are fairly clear: it would generate a much more detailed picture of the nuclear sector in the country concerned and give the IAEA a very solid basis for drawing conclusions about the exclusively peaceful nature of nuclear activities. The main drawback of such an approach is usually considered to be that a reduction in flexibility could deprive states of options that might prove useful under certain circumstances. This can be illustrated with the example of North Korea, where the effort to rein in a nuclear programme of great concern was based in part on supplying North Korea with controlled items during what can now be seen as the period of highest proliferation risk.

An objective application of criteria in a nuclear export licensing assessment would have led to the complete exclusion of North Korea from international nuclear commerce after 1993. However, a system of incentives in which nuclear technology transfers played a prominent part (the 1994 Agreed Framework) became a central element in the international effort to persuade North Korea to move back from its nuclear weapon programme.[165]

After the North Korean–US talks in Pyongyang in October 2002, the publication of information related to uranium enrichment activities in North Korea triggered a series of events that led to an IAEA finding that further violations of the country's safeguards agreement had occurred. In December 2002 IAEA inspectors and safeguards-related equipment were removed from North Korea. Taken in conjunction with other developments (including the country's withdrawal from the NPT in 2003) this convinced many observers that North Korea was making a dedicated effort to acquire nuclear weapons. This was confirmed in October 2006 when North Korea carried out a nuclear test explosion. The UN Security Council subsequently adopted Resolution 1718 on 14 October 2006.[166] It requires UN members to 'prevent

---

[165] In Oct. 1994 North Korea and the USA signed the Agreed Framework, a non-legally binding undertaking that specified certain obligations for the respective parties as well as joint obligations. As part of the Agreed Framework the USA agreed to cooperate with North Korea on the replacement of North Korea's graphite-moderated reactors and related facilities with 2 light-water reactor power plants. Under the Agreed Framework the USA also undertook to organize an international consortium which would have delivered equipment, fuel and other controlled items to North Korea. For the Agreed Framework and other relevant documents see <http://www.kedo.org/>.

[166] The decisions taken by the UN Security Council are discussed further in Anthony and Bauer (note 50), pp. 658–63.

the direct or indirect supply, sale or transfer to the DPRK, through their territories or by their nationals, or using their flag vessels or aircraft, and whether or not originating in their territories' of a range of different items. The resolution also bans the supply of major conventional weapons and of items set out in three lists that accompany the resolution. These three lists correspond to the lists developed and adopted by the Australia Group, the Missile Technology Control Regime and the NSG.[167] The resolution also bans the provision of technical training, advice, services or assistance related to embargoed items.

The UN Security Council took the view that special measures were called for after North Korea's nuclear test. However, the measures contained in Security Council Resolution 1718 were presented as targeted and limited measures integrated into a package that included a dialogue on nuclear issues with North Korea. This overall package could contain rewards in the event that it proved fruitful. Adopting the general condition that only states that have signed an Additional Protocol to their safeguards agreement with the IAEA would be allowed to import equipment for their civilian nuclear programmes might raise an additional barrier to a 'package deal' aimed at addressing proliferation concerns in North Korea or potentially in other countries as well.

A further concern is that the development and application of very restrictive guidelines by the NSG's members would stimulate the development of new sources of nuclear technology and material that are no longer available from traditional suppliers. Alternatively, suppliers that had previously looked inward, supplying their own domestic market exclusively, might be encouraged to look outward in search of new markets in other countries. This may compound a trend that some analysts already anticipate—shortage of uranium enrichment capacity after the year 2015. Thomas Neff, a senior researcher at the Center for International Studies at the Massachusetts Institute of Technology, has written that existing and planned uranium and enrichment production capacity would be almost sufficient to fuel reactors that are currently operating throughout their lifetime. However, Neff also wrote that this capacity 'is far from enough to fuel the

---

[167] The items covered are battle tanks, armoured combat vehicles, large-calibre artillery systems, combat aircraft, attack helicopters, warships, and missiles or missile systems as defined for the purpose of the UN Register of Conventional Arms (UNROCA). On UNROCA see <http://disarmament.un.org/cab/register.html>.

expanded fleet of the nuclear renaissance in 2015. To provide this additional fuel, we must look to potential additional uranium and enrichment'.[168]

There is evidence that some companies in NSG participating states are already anticipating this shortfall in enrichment capacity and working to meet it. For example, in Australia an innovative laser technology with commercial applications in uranium enrichment has been developed by a company called Silex Systems Limited. In May 2006 Silex signed a licensing agreement for the commercialization of this technology with the US-based company General Electric (GE).[169] According to Silex chief executive officer (CEO) Michael Goldsworthy, this was a 'defining moment for Silex Systems' because 'while Silex developed the technology concept, GE has the required technological and commercial capabilities to take it to the next level and beyond'.[170] The president and CEO of GE's nuclear branch, Andy White, added, 'by acquiring the exclusive rights to complete the development and commercial deployment of Silex's enrichment technology, GE will be in a strong position to support anticipated demands for enriched uranium'.[171]

A number of countries outside the NSG have developed a technological and industrial base covering large parts of the nuclear fuel cycle. There are companies and facilities in these states that could offer controlled items to customers in countries that do not have an Additional Protocol and who therefore cannot import from NSG participating states.

Examples of countries that do not participate in the NSG but that either have or are developing significant domestic nuclear industries are India, Iran, Israel, North Korea and Pakistan. As of June 2007, 82 states—as well as the European Atomic Energy Community (Euratom)—had Additional Protocols in force. However, the list of states where the Additional Protocol is not yet in force includes not only Iran and North Korea but also others that are of potential signifi-

[168] Neff, T., 'Uranium and enrichment: fuel for the nuclear renaissance', *Nuclear Energy Review*, no. 41 (Dec. 2006), p. 42.

[169] However, experts have suggested that commercial-scale deployment of the Silex technology will take a minimum of 10 years. Australian Government, Department of the Prime Minister and Cabinet, 'Uranium mining, processing and nuclear energy review', <http://www.pmc.gov.au/umpner/index.cfm>.

[170] 'GE partners with laser enricher Silex', *Nuclear Engineering International*, 23 May 2006, <http://www.neimagazine.com/story.asp?sc=2036249>.

[171] 'GE partners with laser enricher Silex' (note 170).

cance from a non-proliferation perspective. There could be a risk that by tightening its own guidelines the NSG might create new opportunities for international nuclear cooperation among non-members.

Finally, a practical problem for the tightening of guidelines is the question of whether existing NSG participating states are themselves willing to comply with restrictions that they impose on others as a condition of supply. As of May 2007, two NSG participants (Argentina and Brazil) had not taken any steps to discuss an Additional Protocol with the IAEA, and several others had not brought agreements into force. According to public reports, Argentina and Brazil have argued that any link to the Additional Protocol should be voluntary, while Russia and at least one other country have argued that the link to the Additional Protocol should only apply to transfers of enrichment and reprocessing capacities.[172]

Although there are potential risks involved with making the Additional Protocol a new condition of supply, the idea is endorsed by many NSG participating states. The leaders of the G8 group of industrialized states have determined that the Additional Protocol 'must become an essential new standard in the field of nuclear supply arrangements' and have committed themselves to work to strengthen NSG Guidelines accordingly.[173] The EU has also made a commitment to work towards making the Additional Protocol a condition of supply.[174]

Although strengthening of the NSG Guidelines is not without some difficulties, a general tendency is emerging for the Additional Protocols to be seen as an integral part of the IAEA safeguards system. Therefore, in future, adopting an Additional Protocol is likely to be considered an essential aspect of demonstrating compliance with Article III of the NPT and an essential tool for detecting violations of the NPT. The use of the Additional Protocol as a condition of supply seems inevitable, but exactly how this commitment will be incorporated into the NSG Guidelines is less clear.

---

[172] Boese, W., 'US nuclear trade restriction initiatives still on hold', *Arms Control Today*, Dec. 2004.

[173] G8 (note 16).

[174] Statement by H. E. Mr. Richard Ryan, Ambassador, Permanent Representative of Ireland to the United Nations, on behalf of the European Union, in the General Debate, Third Session of the Preparatory Committee for the 2005 Review Conference of the Parties to the Treaty on the Non-Proliferation of Nuclear Weapons, New York, 26 Apr. 2004, <http://www.europa-eu-un.org/articles/en/article_3439_en.htm>.

Limiting the spread of the most proliferation-sensitive technologies

The US proposal, made by President Bush in his 2004 speech at the National Defense University, to deny the transfer of items associated with the most sensitive parts of the nuclear fuel cycle to states that do not already possess such capacities has since been discussed at length in the NSG. However not all participating states seem likely to support it. After the demand for nuclear energy-generating capacity stalled in the 1980s, the global surplus in nuclear fuel production capacity militated against an expansion in the number of uranium enrichment facilities. However, the lack of support for the proposal reflects an unwillingness to close off options in the light of changing assessments of the future demand for nuclear energy. A growing number of countries may become engaged in commercial activities that are proliferation-sensitive, perhaps including uranium enrichment.

As noted above, Australia—an NSG participating state and the world's main exporter of uranium—has decided to pursue commercialization of uranium enrichment technology in partnership with the USA after carrying out a review of future options for the nuclear industry. Australia has also held discussions on the future prospects for the nuclear industry with Canada, the world's second largest producer of uranium.[175] It is possible that other important uranium-producing countries, such as Kazakhstan and Ukraine, will also see commercial merits in investing in new technical capacities, depending on the future prospects for nuclear energy generation.

If a prohibition on the further spread of the most sensitive items cannot be agreed, then additional objective criteria could provide a common guide to thinking about how guidelines could be applied to the most sensitive items. This might be preferable to the current situation, in which states individually interpret the non-proliferation principle in the NSG Guidelines.

The main purpose of civilian nuclear trade is to support electricity generation, and countries that have developed or are examining the development of sensitive nuclear fuel-cycle activities, notably uranium enrichment, have cited energy policy and energy requirements as the reason for doing so. One useful element to guide exporting states could be an agreed method for evaluating whether the potential recipi-

---

[175] Australian Government (note 169).

ent has a credible nuclear power generation programme and justified related nuclear fuel-cycle requirements.

At least one non-governmental study has elaborated criteria that could be used to judge the need for national ownership of uranium enrichment facilities. The study, undertaken at Princeton University, suggested that a country should have or plan to have at least 10 gigawatts of light-water electricity generating capacity in order to qualify to host sensitive facilities. This level of capacity would generate domestic demand at a level high enough to compete with existing enrichment facilities.[176] However, establishing this criterion would disqualify two countries with existing enrichment plants (Brazil and the Netherlands) while enabling the establishment of commercial uranium enrichment facilities in four additional countries (Germany, Japan, South Korea and Ukraine).[177]

The case of Iran serves to illustrate the problems of developing a common approach to assessing the legitimacy of a country's claim to use nuclear imports to support its energy policy. On the face of it, reaching a common position would seem straightforward, but there are underlying complications.

According to Iran's official statements, the main priority of its nuclear programme is the generation of electricity. Two elements are said to have disrupted the Iranian national energy strategy based on fossil resources: first, rising living standards and improvement of economic indicators have prompted an increase in the demand for energy in domestic and industrial sectors; and second, the Iranian economy has become dependent on oil revenues. A long-term strategy to produce electricity in nuclear power plants has been explained as necessary to help meet demand while releasing oil resources for sale to raise foreign currency. This strategy includes a plan to construct nuclear power plants to generate 7000 megawatts of electricity by 2020.[178]

---

[176] Habib, B. et al., *Stemming the Spread of Enrichment Plants: Fuel-Supply Guarantees and the Development of Objective Criteria for Restricting Enrichment* (Woodrow Wilson School of Public and International Affairs, Princeton University: Princeton, N.J., Jan. 2006), <http:// www.princeton.edu/~globsec/academics/>.

[177] The authors of the Princeton University study acknowledge this potential difficulty but regard it as manageable.

[178] The main point of reference for Iranian plans is the speech by Aghazadeh, R., Vice-President of Iran, 'Iran's nuclear policy: peaceful, transparent, independent', Presented to the IAEA, Vienna, 6 May 2003.

Iran intends to develop and build several different reactor types, including heavy water moderated reactors, additional pressurized light water reactors and research reactors, in order to have a programme as reliant on local capabilities and human resources as possible. Iran views the attainment of self-sufficiency in nuclear fuel supply as a necessary part of its policy of self-reliance. According to Iranian officials, the decision to build different types of nuclear power plant creates the need to develop different types of nuclear fuel, which from Iran's perspective means self-sufficiency in the whole 'front end' of the nuclear fuel cycle, including producing the feedstock for uranium enrichment and the capability to enrich uranium.[179]

However, US Vice-President Dick Cheney summarized the question many analysts have posed when he noted that Iran is 'already sitting on an awful lot of oil and gas. Nobody can figure why they need nuclear as well to generate energy'.[180] A number of observers have questioned whether Iran's economic arguments in support of an increased role for nuclear power are credible given the current global surplus of enriched uranium. The costs to Iran of developing the infrastructure needed to develop, build and support power plants far outweigh the value of the electricity generated. Moreover, a number of studies have noted that Iran could not achieve energy independence with its current strategy because confirmed uranium resources in Iran are not sufficient to support the announced programme over the lifetime of planned reactors.[181]

The long-term economic arguments in favour of using nuclear power as part of a broad energy strategy are more difficult to analyse and reach conclusions about. In light of a study made by the Parliamentary Office of Science and Technology (POST), the British House of Commons concluded in 2004 that 'the arguments as to whether Iran has a genuine requirement for domestically-produced nuclear electricity are not all, or even predominantly, on one side'.[182]

---

[179] Kile, ed. (note 126), pp. 2–4.

[180] 'Iran: arguments just don't square up', *Washington Post*, 27 Mar. 2005.

[181] Milazzo, M. and Wood, T., 'Economic analysis of the Iranian nuclear fuel cycle', *Global Security*, vol. 2, no. 3 (spring 2006), p. 6.

[182] Cope, D. R., Director of POST, 'The role of nuclear in a mix of electricity generation: the case of Iran', Memorandum submitted by the Foreign Affairs and Commonwealth Office to the Select Committee on Foreign Affairs, 19 Mar. 2004, <http://www.publications. parliament.uk/pa/cm200304/cmselect/ cmfaff/80/80we02.htm>

The POST analysis concludes that there may be some merit to several of the Iranian arguments in favour of expanding the nuclear sector. The analysis also points out the growing complexity of evaluating other aspects of the arguments made by Iran. These include the rationale that diversification away from fossil fuels will reduce the amount of greenhouse gases emitted in the future (and possibly other environmental impacts), and a consideration of the economic impact of taking away state subsidies for domestic electricity consumption.

Not only Iran, but also a number of other countries are re-evaluating their long-term national energy strategies, including the proper role of nuclear power. The Australian Government's nuclear energy review examined, among other things, how and in what circumstances nuclear energy could be economically attractive to the country in the longer term.[183] The Australian approach was also partly guided by the conviction that 'global energy demand, driven by China, India and the developing world, will explode in coming decades and Australia, holding possibly the largest reserves of uranium in the world, has a national interest and global responsibility in this process'.[184]

It is not known how Argentina and South Africa—two countries that previously developed uranium enrichment capacities largely for reasons of proliferation, but decided to give them up—will respond in the changing commercial environment for the nuclear sector. Against this backdrop, a country such as Iran can present a decision not to close-off future options with regard to nuclear power generation as being consistent with a widespread emerging tendency to explore enrichment capacity to meet future international as well as national demand. Countries might apply a similar rationale in support of the development of facilities to manage the 'back end' of the nuclear fuel cycle, in that the management of nuclear waste might in the future become a commercially worthwhile activity.

It can be concluded from this that efforts by the NSG to develop a methodology to evaluate the role of nuclear power in future energy strategy would be worthwhile, and could contribute to a more effective and more harmonized approach to applying the non-proliferation principle. However, it can also be seen that developing such a methodology would by no means be straightforward.

---

[183] Australian Government (note 169).
[184] Kelly, P., 'A debate we can't put off', *The Australian*, 24 May 2006.

Multinational involvement as a condition of supply

If enrichment or reprocessing facilities, equipment or technology are to be transferred, suppliers should encourage recipients to accept, as an alternative to national plants, supplier involvement or other appropriate foreign participation in resulting facilities. This should be differentiated from proposals that involve either the conversion of existing national nuclear facilities to facilities that are under multinational ownership or operation, or the construction of new joint facilities.[185]

Suppliers could also promote international (including IAEA) activities concerned with multinational regional fuel-cycle centres. By increasing transparency and building confidence between countries at the regional level these arrangements help reduce the risk of proliferation. In this way they can also provide reassurance to suppliers that controlled items will not be diverted or misused. There are examples of regional arrangements where certain aspects of nuclear regulation are organized through international bodies (see section IV).

Other suggestions for revised conditions of supply

The NSG participating states exchange information about export applications that have been denied by national authorities in other participating states on the grounds that the particular export would be inconsistent with the NSG objectives and rules. The authority that issued the original denial will have concluded that the export would be inconsistent with the objectives of the NSG. Partners should not 'undercut' this denial without a good reason and an NSG partner is already required to consult with the country that issued a denial if it is considering an application to make an essentially identical export. Nonetheless, after such consultation the national authority may decide nonetheless to authorize the export.

Going ahead with an export in the face of a denial by an NSG partner might reflect the different level of information available to export authorities or the provision of additional assurances by the importing state or the end-user. However, one option for the NSG might be to modify the guidelines to take away the discretion of national export authorities to undercut a denial by an NSG partner. The risk that a frivolous denial could be issued as a tool to prevent nuclear supply by

---

[185] Proposals of this kind appear in IAEA, INFCIRC/640, 22 Feb. 2005.

a partner in the NSG could be reduced by introducing a rule that an export may not be authorized if it has been the subject of a denial by more than one participating state.

The NSG Guidelines require states to deny authorization of exports unless the end-user has made a commitment to the supplier to apply mutually agreed physical protection measures that conform to international standards. This is intended to reduce any risk of materials or sensitive items being diverted from the end-use that was stated in the export application. The fact that the IAEA has established agreed technical standards for physical protection that are a recognized reference point for nuclear industries worldwide has made it easier to agree the physical protection condition of supply.

However, despite these measures there is still a risk that imported items can be re-exported by the consignee after some period without any assessment of the new end-user. Therefore, a sensible modification to the NSG Guidelines would be to stipulate that exports would only be authorized to countries that have a demonstrated commitment to effective export control and that the export control system of the importing country conforms to the highest international standards.

The NSG Guidelines already contain some conditions that are indirectly linked to the export control system of the importing state. Before transferring trigger list items NSG participating states should seek an assurance that any re-transfer will only take place if the recipient of the re-transfer provides the same assurances as the original recipient in regard to the item concerned. The consent of the supplier should be sought before the re-transfer of any trigger list item or any nuclear dual-use item. In the case of trigger list items the supplier should obtain government-to-government agreement that this consent will be sought as a condition of the original transfer.

Unlike the case of physical protection, there is no internationally agreed technical standard for export controls. The current guidelines do not require the supplier to satisfy itself that an importing state has the legal and administrative system in place to give effect to re-transfer commitments. Under these conditions, it would be reasonable for NSG participating states to regard the standards developed by the NSG itself as the highest international standard. The guidelines could therefore state that exports would only be authorized to countries that can show that their national export control systems conform to NSG standards. An even stricter approach might be that exports would only be authorized to states that align themselves formally with the NSG. This could have the effect of spreading the standards established by the NSG without expanding participation in the group.

In the process of facilitating the implementation of UN Security Council Resolution 1540 the experts supporting the 1540 Committee have compiled detailed information about national laws, regulations and procedures on a range of issues relevant to the operative provisions of the resolution, including export controls.[186] This information, collected from governments and validated by them, could provide the basis for a judgement about whether states meet an acceptable export control standard. The information published by the UN has underlined that the systems of export control in place in countries that import nuclear items on the NSG control list leave a lot to be desired.

To illustrate, Iran reported on the status of its laws on export control and border security in its report to the 1540 Committee. Iran has a 1971 Law on Customs Affairs that bans the export of arms from Iran to non-state actors. Iran also has a 1974 law laying down penalties for the smuggling of arms. The 1997 Islamic Penal Code established penalties for environmental pollution arising from the use of chemical and biological weapons. This appears to be the total legal basis for controlling weapons of mass destruction in Iran.

According to the Iranian report to the UN two bills are pending before the Iranian Parliament. One is to establish a national law to implement the 1993 Chemical Weapons Convention[187], and the other is to establish a law on terrorism. From this it can be seen that even if current legislative plans are fulfilled Iran will be a very long way from establishing export controls that meet the standards applied in NSG participating states.

III. Country-specific nuclear export controls

An alternative way to approach the question of strengthening the NSG Guidelines would be to differentiate between countries for purposes of applying existing guidelines or to require specific countries to cross

---

[186] On the 1540 Committee see <http://disarmament2.un.org/Committee1540/>.

[187] The Convention on the Prohibition of the Development, Production, Stockpiling and Use of Chemical Weapons and on their Destruction was signed on 13 Jan. 1993 and entered into force on 29 Apr. 1997.

higher thresholds than others in order to qualify as partners in nuclear cooperation and trade.

While the system of exchanging information related to licence denials combined with the 'no-undercut' policy creates a de facto list of commercial entities that are treated with extreme caution, Carlton Thorne noted in 1997 that in the NSG 'there are no secret lists of "bad guy" countries'.[188] For the first part of the life of the NSG (which from the outset included participating states from either side of the cold war ideological divide) a list of target countries would have been extremely unlikely.

After the adoption of the guidelines in September 1977 the NSG did not meet again until 1991. Moreover, the identification of countries such as India or Israel by name would almost certainly have been politically unacceptable to one or more of the NSG partners. At the same time, during the cold war there was a strong (albeit tacit) consensus among otherwise adversarial cold war rivals on the need to prevent further nuclear weapon proliferation because that could disturb international strategic stability and might, in case of a crisis, lead to unpredictable consequences given the nuclear stand-off between the superpowers.

After the end of the cold war this consensus came under pressure as the strategic environment changed in ways that reduced the risk of a global nuclear crisis, while nuclear exports remained potentially highly lucrative and at least one important nuclear exporter—Russia—was facing a severe economic downturn. This change made it impossible to reorient COCOM-type controls and apply prohibitions on nuclear supply to new target countries.

The level of current concern about nuclear proliferation may have changed the environment again to the point where it could become possible to agree on a common approach to export controls based on calibrating the degree of risk presented by different countries. According to this logic, states might be sorted into categories. Some states have past and current activities and behaviour that could make them

[188] Thorne (note 41), p. 2. During the cold war a different export control cooperation arrangement—COCOM—did focus on an agreed list of countries. In effect, COCOM established an embargo on transfers of listed items (including nuclear and nuclear-related items) to the Soviet Union and its allies from which exceptions could be granted on a case-by-case basis and only with the agreement of all COCOM partners. There was discussion in the early 1990s on modifying COCOM to maintain the same form of controls but on a different group of countries. It was not possible to agree on such a change and COCOM was dissolved in 1995.

such sensitive destinations from a proliferation standpoint that little if any nuclear commerce with them could be justified. Conversely, there are states with no past or current history of questionable behaviour that neither have nor seek to control the most sensitive parts of the nuclear fuel cycle and that have effective systems to reduce any risk of diversion or unauthorized re-export. Provided that these countries are willing to be transparent and accountable regarding domestic measures that reduce the risk of trafficking, they might in theory form a 'white list' for which the use of simplified licensing procedures could be envisaged for exports of dual-use items.

As evidence for a change in thinking within the NSG it can be noted that, since 2002, the group has somewhat modified its traditional policy of not mentioning countries of concern by name. At an extraordinary plenary meeting of the NSG held in December 2002 'to respond to the new proliferation and security challenges' the NSG participating states called on all states 'to exercise extreme vigilance that their exports and any goods or nuclear technologies that transit their territorial jurisdiction do not contribute to any aspect of a North Korean nuclear weapons effort'.[189] This tendency continued at the NSG plenary in Gothenburg, Sweden, in May 2004 when participating states considered suspending the supply of nuclear items to any state found to be in non-compliance with the NPT or obligations under its safeguards agreement with the IAEA. While stopping short of naming Iran directly in this context, the participating states did refer in their public documents to the findings of the Board of Governors of the IAEA regarding Iran.[190]

One argument in favour of using country lists to raise the efficiency of export controls is that it can reduce the number of cases where a thorough assessment is needed prior to issuing a decision on a given export licence application. This would free the majority of available resources within the licensing system to concentrate on those cases in which risk assessment is more difficult. In cases where NSG participating states agreed on a strong presumption of denial or a prohibition on exports to a 'blacklisted' destination, the task of a licensing officer

---

[189] Press statement from the Nuclear Suppliers Group extraordinary plenary meeting, Vienna, 13 Dec. 2002, <http://www.sipri.org/contents/expcon/nsg_plenary0212.html>.

[190] NSG plenary statement 2004, 'The NSG: strengthening the nuclear non-proliferation regime', NSG plenary meeting, Gothenburg, Sweden, 27–28 May 2004, <http://www.sipri.org/contents/expcon/nsg_plenary 04.html>.

receiving such an application from an exporter would be fairly straightforward.

Using a country list as the basis for export control might also simplify the task of authorities responsible for the enforcement of controls. Customs authorities may find it difficult to identify nuclear dual-use items that require an export licence purely on the basis of technical characteristics of the items concerned. This would require a level of knowledge of the technical aspects of export control lists that few customs officers can reasonably be expected to have acquired. However, in cases where exports are to a blacklisted country, customs officers would know to stop all outbound shipments for closer inspection.

The record of enforcement in the respective cases of Iraq and North Korea during the 1990s illustrates the advantages of country-specific restrictions. North Korea has been judged by the IAEA to be in violation of its safeguards agreement with the agency (which entered into force in 1992) since April 1993. At that time serious discrepancies had been identified between the baseline declaration of fissile materials by North Korea and the results of IAEA inspections. In spite of the grave concerns about its nuclear programme after 1993, North Korea was not subject to comprehensive sanctions or a trade embargo. It is difficult to know the degree to which foreign suppliers (including those within NSG participating states) have transferred nuclear and nuclear dual-use items to North Korea. A country report compiled for the non-governmental, but authoritative, Nuclear Threat Initiative includes a number of unconfirmed reports about foreign support to the nuclear programme in North Korea by individuals and entities from four NSG participating states—Germany, Japan, Russia and Ukraine—during the 1980s and 1990s.[191] An unclassified Central Intelligence Agency (CIA) report noted that North Korea began seeking centrifuge-related materials in large quantities in 2001 and also 'obtained equipment suitable for use in uranium feed and withdrawal systems'.[192]

One option for the NSG would be to develop country-specific export controls to be applied to any recipient that has ever been

[191] Nuclear Threat Initiative, 'North Korea profile: nuclear', <http://www.nuclearthreat initiative.org/e_research/profiles/NK/Nuclear/46.html>.

[192] CIA, 'Report to Congress on the acquisition of technology relating to weapons of mass destruction and advanced conventional munitions covering the period January–June 2002', Apr. 2003, <https://www.cia.gov/library/reports/archived-reports-1/jan_jun2002.html>.

reported by the IAEA Secretariat to the Board of Governors as being in breach of its safeguards agreement, as was the case with North Korea in 1993. The country-specific controls might be in the form of a prohibition on supply of controlled items (or a narrower range of particularly sensitive items). The restrictions might also be calibrated by placing additional restrictions on supply according to the response of the target country to the IAEA allegations and the extent to which corrective measures are taken to address problems identified in IAEA reporting. This approach of developing country-specific export controls could be carried out autonomously by the NSG. However, such an approach might be only one element in a wider set of measures intended to address an identified nuclear programme of concern.

After August 1990 Iraq was subject to a mandatory arms embargo (imposed under UN Security Council Resolution 660 of 2 August 1990) and then to full economic sanctions that included a ban on trade in a wide spectrum of items that could contribute to nuclear, biological or chemical weapon programmes or delivery systems for such weapons. This comprehensive embargo appears to have been highly successful in preventing any Iraqi procurement for its nuclear programme. After 1995, when the Security Council began to relax the embargo on Iraq somewhat, the volume of trade with Iraq increased. The UN established an export–import mechanism in 1996 to monitor this trade in order to reduce the risk that Iraq would acquire proliferation-sensitive items under the new arrangements.[193]

After the new export–import mechanism began, UN inspectors almost immediately began to observe procurement by various Iraqi facilities of declarable dual-use items and materials outside the scope of the embargo. After UN inspectors were forced to leave in 1998, Iraq began to rebuild its procurement system. According to the UN Monitoring, Verification and Inspection Commission (UNMOVIC), by 2002 Iraq had rebuilt and further developed its procurement network for the acquisition of foreign materials, equipment and technology by creating a network of state-owned trading companies established and controlled by a Military Industrialization Commission

with branches in foreign countries; the Iraqi private sector and foreign trading companies operating in Iraq and abroad; multiple intermediaries; chains

[193] The mechanism was established under UN Security Council Resolution 1051, 27 Mar. 1996.

of foreign suppliers of items and materials; bank accounts; and transport-ation companies. In several instances, the Iraqi state-owned trading com-panies had shares in foreign trading companies or were closely affiliated with local private trading companies but using private trading companies that in turn established cooperation networks with foreign, private trading companies.[194]

In this way Iraq acquired items and materials about which it should have notified the UN about but did not.

The risk that Iraq will acquire nuclear weapons has been effectively eliminated by the removal of the regime of Saddam Hussein and the occupation of the country by the armed forces of the USA and its coa-lition partners. However, IAEA inspectors were able to return to Iraq in December 2002. During the four months before the invasion of Iraq in March 2003, the IAEA found no signs that the nuclear weapon pro-gramme had been restarted. While the IAEA did not recommend clos-ing the nuclear file on Iraq in its reports to the UN Security Council prior to the occupation, in July 2004 the new government of Iraq requested the return of IAEA inspectors as part of the process of pre-paring a final report on the non-presence of nuclear weapons in Iraq—one of the preconditions for the lifting of remaining UN sanctions.

The country-specific controls placed on Iraq were effective because they were embedded in a wider system of UN sanctions that obliged all countries to be extremely vigilant in monitoring any exports where Iraq was the final destination. The sanctions system was supported by extensive monitoring around the borders of Iraq carried out by the armed forces of a number of states (led by the USA). Moreover, in the period 1991–98 the IAEA was conducting inspections at nuclear sites in Iraq where any items imported illegally might have been detected. Taken together, these measures strengthened the enforcement of export controls.

The alternative approach of using a 'white list' as the basis for a system of simplified controls has been proposed periodically, often by industry associations. For example, during the preparation of the first regulation establishing an EU dual-use export control system, the European Chemical Industry Council (CEFIC) proposed that an end-user located in any country participating in all four of the export con-trol cooperation arrangements (the Australia Group, the Missile Tech-

---

[194] United Nations Monitoring, Verification and Inspection Commission, Note by the Secretary-General, United Nations Security Council document S/2006/420, 21 June 2006.

nology Control Regime, the NSG and the Wassenaar Arrangement) should be eligible to receive controlled items under a general licence.[195] The EU has in effect created a white list in an annex to its Council Regulation 1334/2000, the primary legislation that controls exports of dual-use items and that is binding on all EU member states.[196] Annex II of the regulation lists seven countries to which most dual-use items subject to control (including many nuclear dual-use items) may be exported using a Community General Export Authorization (CGEA). The seven countries are Australia, Canada, Japan, New Zealand, Norway, Switzerland and the United States. The CGEA is a general licence that pre-authorizes the export of dual-use items to the listed countries with certain exceptions that are specified in the regulation. Exporters must register the use of the licence with the competent authorities when exporting controlled items but need not apply for permission to export since it has already been granted in the CGEA.

Although there is some experience with using both blacklists and white lists, the decision about how countries should be classified may not be straightforward. For example, Brazil has a chequered nuclear history, having actively investigated a nuclear weapon option in the fairly recent past.[197] At the same time, Brazil is a member of the NSG and has developed a cooperative relationship with the IAEA. Brazil has taken on commitments in the regional context as well as signing and ratifying the NPT. Brazil has also signed and ratified the CTBT.

In 2002 the Brazilian Government announced that Brazil was conducting a uranium enrichment programme to produce fuel for two nuclear power plants and for export within a decade. In the past Brazil has developed enrichment technologies on a limited scale for research purposes but has purchased enriched uranium for fuel fabrication from suppliers in Europe. According to the 2002 government statement, the new programme would not only guarantee Brazil a secure domestic supply of enriched uranium but would also be the basis for exports of enriched uranium to other countries after approximately 2014.

---

[195] CEFIC, 'CEFIC comments on the draft Council Regulation on the control of exports of certain dual-use goods and technologies and of certain nuclear products and technologies', CEFIC Position Paper, 16 Sep. 1992, <http://www.cefic.be/position/Tea/pp_tm009.htm>.

[196] Council Regulation (EC) no. 1334/2000 (note 9).

[197] Feldman, Y., 'Country profile 11: Brazil', <http://www.sipri.org/contents/expcon/cnsc1bra.html>.

The first of four planned modules of the Resende uranium facility was inaugurated in May 2006.[198] In 2003 the IAEA was negotiating with the Brazilian Government to ensure that the new facility was subject to safeguards before beginning operations. However, significant parts of the facility were shrouded by newly built walls and coverings when IAEA inspectors visited the plant in February and March 2004. The Brazilian Government agreed that inspectors would be allowed access only after specific language had been negotiated in its agreement with the IAEA to protect industrial secrets.

The IAEA has not expressed doubts about the non-nuclear weapon status of Brazil. However, the enrichment programme and the discussions between the IAEA and Brazil over safeguards have been interpreted by some analysts as evidence of a possible tendency for states to pursue a 'hedge' strategy, building a technological and industrial base that keeps open the option of acquiring nuclear weapons in future. Under these circumstances the question arises how a country like Brazil would be treated in conditions where country lists played a more prominent part in export assessments.

IV. A global framework regulating nuclear supply

Although in 2004 the IAEA Director General proposed the establishment of 'binding, treaty-based controls' to regulate the supply of proliferation-sensitive nuclear items, ElBaradei did not provide any details of what such a system would look like.[199] The intention behind his statement was likely to have been to stimulate discussion and debate, as there are reasons to doubt whether such a global system could be established in the short term.

Over time a global system could be built by continuously expanding participation in the NSG. The NSG has expanded gradually since 1991, when there were 22 participating states (see table 2.1). In June 2004, China, Estonia, Lithuania and Malta joined the NSG and in June 2005 Croatia became the 45th NSG participating state. Continuing to expand the NSG to take in additional nuclear suppliers is an option that has not been excluded by the participating states. Moreover, until it joined the group, China would have been listed as a country whose

---

[198] 'Brazil officially starts first uranium enrichment facility', Environment News Service, 8 May 2006, <http://www.ens-newswire.com/ens/may2006/2006-05-08-04.asp>.
[199] ElBaradei (note 1).

supply policies might undercut the effectiveness of any attempt by the NSG to tighten the restrictions contained in agreed guidelines. In other words, it has been possible to incorporate a 'difficult case' into the NSG. Most of the main nuclear suppliers already participate in the NSG, but expanding the group to include all nuclear suppliers may not be possible and may not even be considered desirable.

Some analysts have asserted that the expansion of the export control cooperation arrangements during the 1990s has already reduced their effectiveness to the point where a radically different solution needs to be found to control international transfers of sensitive items.[200] For example, a recent study by the Center for International Trade and Security (CITS) found that 'many countries have joined the multilateral control regimes even though their security and economic interests differ from those of the original members'.[201] The report also suggests that some new members lack effective national export control systems and hypothesizes that, because trade among regime members is not as carefully scrutinized as trade with those outside the regime, these 'weak links' may be targeted by rogue states and terrorist organizations for exploitation in their efforts to build proscribed weapons.

Continuous expansion might make the practical problem of effective administration of the NSG more difficult. The cost of participation has risen with the expansion in the number of participating states and it is not apparent that states are always willing to meet these costs.[202] During the 1990s there was a significant increase in the amount of information as well as the volume and number of documents exchanged between NSG participating states, all of which needed to be read, evaluated, acted upon and archived nationally. At the same time there has been some evidence that the quality of the information being exchanged within the NSG has become more general and its practical value in implementing export controls may therefore be declining. In particular, there is less willingness to share information about end-users and questionable supply activities—which is the most sensitive information but also the most useful to licensing authorities.

---

[200] Mallik (note 11), p. 123.

[201] Beck, M. et al., *Strengthening Multilateral Export Controls: A Nonproliferation Priority* (University of Georgia, Center for International Trade and Security: Athens, Ga., Sep. 2002), p. 6.

[202] E.g. a number of NSG states did not take part in all of the activities organized under the plenary meeting in Brasilia in 2006, presumably because the cost of participation by a large delegation was not considered justifiable.

There must be a risk that closer cooperation between the multilateral export control regimes would lead to a further watering down of the information exchange.

At present eight countries—China, France, Germany, Japan, the Netherlands, Russia, the UK and the USA—operate one or more industrial-scale uranium enrichment facilities. All of these countries participate in the NSG. Additional industrial-scale facilities are under construction in Brazil, which is an NSG participating state, and Iran, which is not. Furthermore, India and Pakistan—two other states that do not participate in the NSG—have small enrichment facilities associated with their military programmes, and therefore have the knowledge and technical capacity to engage in commercial enrichment should they so decide.

Export controls within a UN framework

There are three ways in which a global legal basis for export control could be established on a comprehensive basis. The first would be in the context of a treaty (either a new treaty or through an amendment of the NPT); the second would be under the authority of the UN Security Council in the framework of Security Council Resolution 1540; and the third would be by giving the task of regulating supply to an empowered agency (which could, but need not, be the IAEA). These approaches are not in theory mutually exclusive and could be designed to be mutually supporting. However, the practical difficulties of achieving such an integrated system are formidable.

A nuclear supply treaty

Through a pragmatic approach of inclusive dialogue, the standards already developed in the NSG about what to control and what factors should guide decisions to authorize or deny exports might, in time, become international standards. If this was to happen, then the universal legal basis for export control called for by the Director General of the IAEA might be possible to agree.

It should be recognized that, although capacities to deliver technical assistance in export control are being developed progressively, at present they remain scarce. The reports provided in the framework of Security Council Resolution 1540 (see below), are likely to help in the more effective targeting of export control assistance to help countries that want to improve their domestic nuclear and dual-use regulations. However, promoting export control standards on a global basis through this approach will inevitably be a long process.

Two US analysts have noted that a treaty could create a verification mechanism, a method of assessing the adequacy of national export control laws and an agreed procedure for investigating alleged cases of illicit trafficking.[203] Discussions on such a treaty might also allay political concerns about expanding the legislative power of the Security Council.

In documents submitted to the 1995 NPT Review and Extension Conference, the Non-Aligned Movement (NAM) underscored the importance of ensuring that export controls do not impede peaceful uses of nuclear energy. It also called for a new ad hoc committee to formulate criteria and procedures for controls on exports to non-nuclear weapon states and to agree on an export control trigger list. This has been interpreted as a reflection of a broad feeling among states that basic standards and practices of export controls should be both designed and implemented on a more multilateral basis. At their October 1995 summit meeting the heads of state and government of the NAM 'noted with concern the growing restraint placed on access to material, equipment and technology for peaceful uses of nuclear energy by the developed countries through imposition of ad-hoc export control regimes'.[204]

The statement by the NAM leaders reflected a concern that export controls may impede economic and social development in developing countries. This point of view has not been accepted by NSG participating states and some have pointed to their own experience of joining the NSG to refute the claim. For example, representatives of Argentina at the 2000 NPT Review Conference stated that accepting the standards of the NSG had not impeded Argentina's capacity to export nuclear products and technologies. On the contrary, effective export controls have facilitated the signature of more than 30 bilateral cooperation agreements on the peaceful uses of nuclear energy, thereby increasing the prospects for economic and social development

---

[203] Albright, D. and Hinderstein, C., 'Unraveling the A. Q. Khan and future proliferation networks', *Washington Quarterly*, vol. 28, no. 2 (spring 2005), p. 126.

[204] NAM Summit Declaration, Cartagena, Colombia, 18–20 Oct. 1995, <http://www.nam.gov.za/xisummit/index.html>

in Argentina.[205] Nevertheless, the concern that the international civilian nuclear market will be manipulated to deter entry by developing countries is likely to be reinforced given the nature of certain current proposals being put forward by NSG participating states.[206] An open and inclusive dialogue on criteria for effective export control might help to reduce this concern. Finally, a treaty establishing conditions for nuclear supply and prescribing standards for export control might offer an avenue for achieving another objective that has been proclaimed by the IAEA Director General:

> to deal creatively with the three countries that remain outside the nuclear Non-Proliferation Treaty (NPT): Pakistan and India, both holders of nuclear arsenals, and Israel, which maintains an official policy of ambiguity but is believed to be nuclear-weapons-capable. ... Our traditional strategy—of treating such states as outsiders—is no longer a realistic method of bringing these last few countries into the fold.[207]

In public statements India, Israel and Pakistan have all made it clear that they want to apply the most modern and effective standards in national export controls. All three have amended their national legislation in line with this commitment. Therefore, these countries could help negotiate a new treaty and, if satisfied with the outcome of the negotiations, sign and ratify it.

UN Security Council Resolution 1540

In September 2003 President Bush urged the UN Security Council to adopt an anti-proliferation resolution calling on all UN member states 'to criminalize the proliferation of weapons of mass destruction, to enact strict export controls consistent with international standards, and to secure any and all sensitive materials within their own borders'.[208]

---

[205] Intervention of Gerardo Bompadre at Main Committee III, 2 May 2000, NPT/CONF. 2000/MC.III/SR.3, 10 May 2000, <http://disarmament.un.org/wmd/npt/srs/2000mc3sr3.htm>.

[206] E.g. 1 element of the Global Nuclar Energy Partnership (GNEP) proposed by the USA in 2006 is to establish a consortium of nations with advanced technologies to enable developing nations to acquire nuclear energy economically while minimizing proliferation risk. In effect this would mean modifying the economic conditions for nuclear supply to deter new entrants. The GNEP is described on the website of the US Department of Energy at <http://www.gnep.energy.gov>.

[207] ElBaradei, M., 'Rethinking nuclear safeguards', *Washington Post*, 14 June 2006.

[208] Address by US President George W. Bush, UN General Assembly 7th Plenary Meeting, New York, N.Y., 23 Sep. 2003, A/58/PV.7., p. 8.

A central argument for developing an anti-proliferation resolution was the difficulty of adapting traditional approaches to non-proliferation in conditions where non-state actors seek access to technologies in order to misuse them. States have found it unfeasible to adapt existing instruments such as the NPT, which has never been revised or updated, for this purpose.

In April 2004 the UN Security Council unanimously adopted Resolution 1540. Unlike most Security Council resolutions, which respond to developments in a particular location, Resolution 1540 has a global application and a preventive character. The evidence of an extensive grey market in nuclear and nuclear-related goods and technologies revealed in information released by the Government of Libya and in investigations carried out by the IAEA was a catalyst for the decision.[209] The urgency of the need to find effective remedies was increased with the discovery of the extent of the activities carried out by the A. Q. Khan network, and this was an additional, powerful catalyst for the discussion and adoption of the resolution.

In Resolution 1540 the UN Security Council, acting under Chapter VII of the UN Charter, mandated a number of steps that states should take to establish and enforce legal barriers to the acquisition of NBC or radiological weapons or nuclear explosive devices, whether by terrorists or by states. Obligations related to export controls feature prominently in the resolution.

Under the terms of the resolution, states 'shall refrain from providing any form of support to non-State actors that attempt to develop, acquire, manufacture, possess, transport, transfer or use nuclear, chemical or biological weapons and their means of delivery', 'shall adopt and enforce appropriate effective laws which prohibit any non-State actor to manufacture, acquire, possess, develop, transport, transfer or use nuclear, chemical or biological weapons and their means of delivery, in particular for terrorist purposes, as well as attempts to engage in any of the foregoing activities, participate in them as an accomplice, assist or finance them' and 'shall take and enforce effective measures to establish domestic controls to prevent the proliferation of nuclear, chemical, or biological weapons and their means of

---

[209] UN, 'A more secure world: our shared responsibility', Report of the High-level Panel on Threats, Challenges and Change', UN document A/59/565 and Corr. 1, 4 Dec. 2004, <http://www.un.org/secureworld/>.

delivery, including by establishing appropriate controls over related materials'.[210]

The resolution also instructs states to put in place some more specific measures necessary to implement it. Accordingly, states are obliged to 'develop and maintain appropriate effective border controls and law enforcement efforts to detect, deter, prevent and combat, including through international cooperation when necessary, the illicit trafficking and brokering in such items in accordance with their national legal authorities and legislation and consistent with international law' and to

establish, develop, review and maintain appropriate effective national export and trans-shipment controls over such items, including appropriate laws and regulations to control export, transit, trans-shipment and re-export and controls on providing funds and services related to such export and trans-shipment such as financing, and transporting that would contribute to proliferation, as well as establishing end-user controls; and establishing and enforcing appropriate criminal or civil penalties for violations of such export control laws and regulations.[211]

Resolution 1540 does not define what would constitute appropriate effective controls and cannot, as currently constructed, be the basis for an international system for regulating nuclear supply. The essential steps that states need to take in order to put in place an effective system must first be defined, but the resolution does provide a basis for assessing the status of export controls currently in place and identifying their main weaknesses that need to be corrected.

Resolution 1540 established a reporting mechanism in the form of a committee of the Security Council consisting of all 15 members. The 1540 Committee has recruited experts to facilitate consideration of national reports submitted by member states and has reported on the contents of those submissions to the Security Council.

At the Security Council discussion of the first information presented by the 1540 Committee it was noted that it was difficult to establish what 'compliance' with the resolution meant in conditions where there was no clear and uniform understanding of what its language was referring to. The existing multilateral agreements referred to in the resolution (including the NPT) do not themselves have universal

---

[210] UN Security Council Resolution 1540 (note 51), Operative paragraphs 1–3.
[211] UN Security Council Resolution 1540 (note 51), Operative paragraph 3.

participation and do not provide detailed guidance about a number of matters. In certain areas (such as nuclear security and the physical security of fissile materials) recognized international standards have been established in the IAEA. However, as regards an effective export control system, no such standards are recognized outside the NSG and the Zangger Committee.

The Security Council could have taken on itself or given the 1540 Committee the task of developing a set of standards to be used as a yardstick when evaluating the effectiveness of measures taken by states to implement the terms of Resolution 1540. However, this would have been controversial against the background of a certain unease expressed by UN member states at the time the resolution was adopted about the Security Council taking on a legislative function on behalf of the international community.

In Resolution 1673 of 27 April 2006 the Security Council renewed the mandate of the 1540 Committee but did not extend it into new areas. It was decided that the 1540 Committee should promote full implementation of Resolution 1540 through a work programme based on compilation of information 'on the status of States' implementation of all aspects of Resolution 1540 (2004), outreach, dialogue, assistance and cooperation'. At the same time, the resolution encouraged 'ongoing dialogue' between the 1540 Committee and states on full implementation, including dialogue 'on further actions needed from States to that end and on technical assistance needed and offered'. Resolution 1673 also invited the 1540 Committee to explore 'with States and international, regional and subregional organizations' (but not with the NSG or the Zangger Committee) experience-sharing and lessons learned in the areas covered by Resolution 1540 and the availability of programmes that might facilitate implementation.

It may be concluded from this that the Security Council is unlikely to prescribe the standards that states should adopt in order to establish appropriate effective export controls. At the same time, the problem remains of how to establish what essential elements are needed in an effective system.

In Resolution 1540 it is anticipated that states in a position to do so would, if requested, offer assistance to states that lack the necessary legal and regulatory infrastructure, implementation experience or resources to meet their obligations. The resolution provides little guidance about how such assistance would be managed. However, under its present format and within its existing mandate the 1540 Committee could develop a document that indicates the essential elements of an appropriate effective export control system. After its establishment, the 1540 Committee received specific offers of technical assistance from the IAEA, the NSG and the Zangger Committee. Discussion with these partners could be a valuable element in elaborating an 'essential elements' document.

The 1540 Committee itself lacks the mandate and the resources for managing a technical assistance programme or linking assistance donors and recipients in specific projects. This task requires a capacity to diagnose the specific problems faced by states and to identify the particular kinds of assistance that potential donors can offer.

A number of states as well as the EU are developing technical assistance programmes that could assist UN members that want to remedy deficiencies in their national export controls. The standards (including control lists and guidelines) promoted through these programmes will in practice be those developed in the Nuclear Suppliers Group. The NSG has increasingly conducted outreach to non-participating states to inform them of developments within the group. Regular meetings between representatives of the NSG, the Zangger Committee, the IAEA, national donors and the European Union as well as the 1540 Committee would be a useful way for those engaged in outreach and assistance to brief themselves on the status of existing activities. This could in turn inform their decisions about where to target outreach and assistance efforts.

A nuclear supply regulatory agency

Iran has proposed in the past that effective transfer guidelines should be developed through multilateral negotiations, which could take place in the IAEA, with the participation of all concerned states, suppliers and recipients.

Under the Additional Protocol there are provisions related to reporting on nuclear exports. States that agree an Additional Protocol with the IAEA must provide the agency with a declaration regarding each export of specified equipment and non-nuclear material listed in an annex to the protocol. For each export the state concerned should report the identity, quantity, location of intended use in the receiving state and the date or expected date of the export.[212] Moreover, if the agency has received information in a declaration by a nuclear exporter it can request confirmation from the importing state and, if the importing state has itself concluded an Additional Protocol, it will be obliged to provide that confirmation.

This information could be extremely valuable to export control authorities. However, it is usually considered to be impossible for the IAEA to share the information gathered during the performance of safeguards-related missions outside the IAEA. The argument for this approach is that if IAEA members thought that the information was being shared they would refuse to provide it and the system of safeguards would collapse. One potential way around the scenario of a separation between comprehensive access to information and the authority to regulate the civilian nuclear sector would be for the IAEA to take on the task of regulation in addition to the task of safeguards and to base both tasks on information accessible internally across the different parts of the agency.

In most countries the regulation of civilian nuclear activities is the legal responsibility of a national authority that normally applies rules based on international standards developed within the framework of the IAEA. There are a number of examples, such as Sweden and the USA, where the nuclear regulatory authority is also partly responsible for nuclear export control, although responsibility is shared with other authorities that control exports of nuclear-related dual-use items. However, multinational arrangements may be one option by which regulation of the nuclear sector could be strengthened. This would involve providing assurances for services that do not involve ownership of facilities.[213] It can be noted that the current NSG Guidelines include language pointing to the potential benefits that could be gained from participation in multinational arrangements to ensure access to nuclear fuel and related services under market conditions.

If this arrangement was under IAEA auspices, it could be achieved through a modification of the Additional Protocol to require prior notification of nuclear transfers and the adoption of a rule by which no

---

[212] IAEA, INFCIRC/540 (note 61), Article 2.ix.a.

[213] This should be differentiated from proposals that involve either the conversion of existing national nuclear facilities to facilities that are under multinational ownership or operation or construction of new joint facilities. There is no theoretical reason why the 2 approaches of multilateral regulation and multilateral ownership should not be applied in parallel. For proposals of this kind see IAEA (note 185).

transfer could take place legally without IAEA authorization. A system of this kind would regulate international transfers and would create new reporting obligations for states since the IAEA deals with national authorities and not directly with nuclear operators. The system would in effect be a transfer of authority from states to the IAEA to give the 'last word' prior to the transfer of a controlled item across a border.

The advantage of such a system would be that through the implementation of the Additional Protocol the IAEA would, over time, develop the most comprehensive database of information about global nuclear facilities. If countries meet their obligations in reporting under the Additional Protocol and if the IAEA is able to link its information internally in an effective way, then the information available to the agency about nuclear activities taking place at individual facilities worldwide would be far in excess of that which would be available to national licensing authorities.

Just as there are examples of regional bodies that work closely with the IAEA to implement safeguards, there may be scope both to develop this approach further in Europe and South America, where it is already being applied, and to initiate new arrangements in other parts of the world.

Under the provisions of the 1957 Treaty establishing the European Atomic Energy Community (the Euratom Treaty),[214] the European Commission acquired the status of a supranational regulatory authority in three functional areas: radiation protection, supply of nuclear fissile materials and nuclear safeguards. Therefore, the administration of EU safeguards has been the responsibility of the European Commission since 1957. Within the Commission, the Directorate-General for Energy and Transport implements safeguards. Whereas the system of safeguards operated by the IAEA depends on information reported by governments, under the Euratom system the Commission works directly with nuclear operators, receiving data from them and with a legal right established in European legislation to inspect sites on the territory of EU member states, including all of the civilian installations of France and the UK. Also under the Euratom Treaty framework, the Euratom Supply Agency is an independent body supervised

---

[214] For the text of the Euratom Treaty see <http://eur-lex.europa.eu/en/treaties/index.htm>.

by the Commission that operates a common nuclear material supply policy throughout the EU.[215]

In South America, Argentina and Brazil developed a system of nuclear safeguards after more than 10 years of confidence building and dialogue on nuclear matters.[216] The Common System for Accounting and Control of Nuclear Materials [Sistema Común de Contabilidad y Control de Materiales Nucleares] (SCCC) was established in November 1990 in a joint declaration, laying the basis for the creation of the Brazilian–Argentine Agency for Accounting and Control of Nuclear Materials [Agencia Brasileño–Argentina de Contabilidad y Control de Materiales Nucleares] (ABACC) in July 1991. Soon thereafter, Brazil, Argentina, ABACC and the IAEA began negotiations on an agreement for application of full-scope safeguards to the nuclear facilities of both countries. In December 1991 the Quadripartite Agreement was concluded among the four parties. It consisted of obligations virtually identical to those under the NPT. ABACC is responsible for verifying the peaceful use of nuclear materials in the two countries and to that end has created a commission and a secretariat. ABACC implements the SCCC, which is applicable to all the nuclear materials used in all the nuclear activities performed within the jurisdictions or in the territories of Argentina and Brazil.[217]

ABACC also works in direct cooperation with nuclear operators and reaches conclusions independent from national authorities in Argentina and Brazil. The SCCC's General Procedures require all facilities to prepare a technical questionnaire containing relevant information on the nuclear material, its use and storage. ABACC then prepares a specific safeguards approach for each facility and prepares an application manual containing procedures tailored to implementing that approach at the specific facility concerned.

As one element of the control system, ABACC must receive the technical questionnaire before the nuclear material reach the facility for the first time. As a general rule, the minimum term fixed is 180 days. As soon as the technical questionnaire is received, ABACC analyses the data and later performs a new analysis of the information

---

[215] On the Euratom Supply Agency see <http://ec.europa.eu/euratom/index_en.html>.

[216] Carasales, J. C., 'The Argentine–Brazilian nuclear rapprochement', *Nonproliferation Review*, no. 3, vol 2 (spring–summer 1995).

[217] The ABACC website documents the development of regional safeguards and bilateral cooperation on nuclear matters between Argentina and Brazil. See <http://www.abacc.org/engl/agreements_statements/index.asp>.

at the facility. After completion of the verification, the IAEA prepares the adequate safeguards approach, which is consolidated in the application manual. After this, the regime of ordinary inspections is enforced for the verification of the nuclear material inventory in that facility and its variations. The results of the evaluation of all the control and verification activities are reported periodically to the corresponding national authority in each country.

The cooperative approach to safeguards in Europe and South America involves countries that are sensitive from a proliferation perspective and engages countries that were former adversaries. This gives the participants a strong self-interest to ensure that commitments are complied with. Neither Euratom nor ABACC is, however, currently charged with prior assessment of nuclear transfers and in each case they coexist with national export controls operated by participating states. However, their direct experience of working with nuclear operators means that within their geographical regions the technical secretariats concerned may have more and better information about what is happening within nuclear facilities and about particular end-users and end-uses than national regulators do.

Allocating further responsibilities to regional bodies would be extremely difficult. Whether the system was organized under IAEA auspices or under regional authorities, tasking multilateral agencies with transfer control would mean addressing the issues of implementation and enforcement.

Within the EU such a system would depend on the willingness of the EU member states (which are responsible for export licensing and enforcement) to ask for the opinion of the Commission before making a decision to grant or deny authorization to export. Creating a centralized system for licensing and enforcement would require a fundamental change in the administration of European export controls.

If a state asked the IAEA for an opinion on applications for export authorization, the decision to approve or deny a licence would still rest with national authorities. This could provide national authorities with an additional layer of assurance. A 'green light' from the IAEA would indicate that the agency had no information suggesting a proliferation risk while a 'red light' would be a strong indication that the national authority should proceed with caution.

A more radical system would be to require IAEA assent before a national authority could grant a 'transaction licence' that is valid in all relevant jurisdictions. This IAEA assent would be based on an overall assessment of the degree of proliferation risk involved in the particular transaction. In future the safeguards system created through Additional Protocols will give the IAEA the most comprehensive picture of the whole supply chain, including both the supply and the demand sides. There could then be a case for a multilateral agency dealing directly with nuclear operators and their industrial suppliers to play a role in an effective transfer control system, while the necessary implementation and enforcement measures would still be the responsibility of states.

In some ways this approach could be better tuned to an increasingly globalized industry where exporters currently face the problem of managing transactions involving partners in several jurisdictions. At present this can require multiple authorizations for the same transaction. The national authorities responsible for assessing export licence applications do not always interpret guidelines and standards in the same way when considering a particular transaction, even if they all participate in the NSG. These different interpretations can be frustrating for industry, which would probably welcome a single licence valid in all of the countries where partners in a given transaction are operating. However, national authorities see export licence assessments as both political and technical decisions and would probably not be willing to give a multilateral agency the power to veto export licences.

V. Strengthening export control enforcement

Export controls criminalize the unauthorized export of specified items and give governments the legal authority to prevent the supply of specified items without a prior assessment of the end-user and the end-use. Enforcing the controls requires governments to work with exporters that intend to comply with existing laws and regulations. Recent proposals to strengthen export controls have emphasized the need to work more closely with industry.[218] Internal controls put in place by exporters are increasingly seen as an important element in

---

[218] The review of dual-use export controls carried out by the EU in 2004 recommended that member states should examine their existing practices on outreach to industry and assess whether improvements should be made. See Council of the European Union, 'Outreach to industry checklist', Council document 15291/05, Brussels, 5 Dec. 2005.

enforcement. However, enforcement operations are also directed at the activities of individuals, companies and entities that try to evade the process of assessment by smuggling controlled items or try to undermine assessments by knowingly submitting partial or false information.

Export controls have traditionally been seen as instruments with which to address the weapon programmes of states. Therefore, export control systems, including enforcement activities, have tended to focus on preventing the unauthorized acquisition of militarily significant quantities of weapons by the armed forces of another country. This approach is reflected in the lists of items subject to control and in the type of information that has been collected on end-users. In recent years, in particular after the attacks on the USA on 11 September 2001, a great deal of attention has been directed to the risk that non-state actors could acquire materials or items that are not normally thought of as weapons. Subsequently, the NSG has given consideration to how it might contribute to counterterrorism. However, the legal framework for export control is likely to change gradually, partly in response to decisions of the UN Security Council.

A reorientation of the legal framework could raise new enforcement issues since a system aimed at counterterrorism might require scrutiny of end-users that were not considered sensitive from a traditional non-proliferation perspective. Moreover, terrorists planning mass impact attacks might also seek items that would not have been seen as weapon-related in the past, for example, materials that could be used in a radiological device (a so-called 'dirty bomb') or very small quantities of material.

Recent events have provided evidence that existing export control laws have not been enforced effectively in NSG participating states. The brief overview of Iraqi procurement efforts during the 1990s offered in section III above underlines how proliferators have adapted their activities to evade export controls by carrying out their acquisitions through a large, dispersed network of operatives, most of whom work at arm's length from the true end-user.[219] Further evi-

---

[219] David Albright has given the example of an Iraqi document from 1986 that advertised Iraqi Atomic Energy Commission lectures at the Al Tuwaitha Nuclear Research Centre on the subject 'deceptive technological policies' to train officials in illicit procurement. Albright, D., 'A commentary on the future of nuclear export controls', Presentation to the Second NSG International Seminar on the Role of Export Controls in Nuclear Non-proliferation, New York, 8–9 Apr. 1999.

dence of shortcomings in enforcement was revealed by recent cases of involvement in illicit trafficking by suppliers located in NSG participating states.

One possible explanation for the failure to enforce export controls has been the low priority that enforcement agencies (which are often the national customs services) attach to the task. Traditionally focused on tasks associated with generating revenue through tax collection and fighting economic crime, many customs services still prioritize these areas rather than their role in strengthening public security by combating proliferation and terrorism. Moreover, many customs services are much better equipped from a technical perspective to recognize and interdict items that were specially designed, developed or adapted for military use than they are for dual-use items. The likelihood that many types of licensable dual-use goods would evade border controls if shipped without an accompanying licence is probably quite high.

The question of effective enforcement of nuclear export controls came to the fore in public discussions in December 2003 after the Libyan Government declared that it would eliminate all materials, equipment and programmes leading to the production of nuclear weapons.[220] Prior to the December announcement Libyan authorities had been holding discussions with officials from the UK and the USA on their nuclear and chemical weapon programmes and missile delivery systems. Following the announcement Libya cooperated proactively with the IAEA to provide information and prompt access to all locations requested by the agency. As a result, these governments and the IAEA came a long way towards gaining a complete picture of the Libyan nuclear programme.

The discussions with Libya (and with Iran in the case of the IAEA) revealed that equipment and technologies had been acquired from a widespread procurement effort and the IAEA found 'increasing evidence of a complex black market network'.[221] The IAEA was not able to state with confidence whether or not sensitive nuclear technologies had also spread through that network to other countries or end-users.

The hub of the international network seems to have been located in Pakistan, rather than in any NSG participating state. It appears that the

---

[220] IAEA, Implementation of the NPT Safeguards Agreement of the Socialist People's Libyan Arab Jamahiriya: report by the IAEA Director General, GOV/2004/12, 20 Feb. 2004.

[221] IAEA, 'IAEA Director General briefs board on Iran, Libya, other topics', IAEA Staff Report, 8 Mar. 2004, <http://www.iaea.org/NewsCenter/News/2004/bog0803.html>.

leading Pakistani scientist A. Q. Khan began to develop a network of procurement specialists and engineers in the 1980s and offered equipment and services to Iran, Libya and, possibly, North Korea. However, it seems that this network also included individuals and companies in Europe that supplied or facilitated the supply of very sensitive technologies such as uranium enrichment capabilities.

In February 2004 the Malaysian police released some details of ongoing investigations of nuclear trafficking activities. The report released included details of activities by individuals from four NSG participating states—Germany, Switzerland, Turkey and the UK.[222] The report also suggests that individuals and companies in France, Italy and Spain may have played some role in the trafficking activities, although the information provided is less specific for these countries. Libya also appears to have sought nuclear items from companies in Finland.[223] In early 2004 authorities in the Netherlands were investigating contacts between at least one Dutch national and the Khan Research Laboratories in Kahuta, Pakistan—believed to be the hub of the nuclear trafficking network. While at the time of writing it is not known whether individuals and companies in NSG participating states broke any law, it is clear that the overall trafficking activities represent a serious challenge to the objectives of nuclear export controls.

Against this background, one important element of the overall discussion of nuclear export control reform is likely to be the question of how to ensure that the activities of exporters are monitored in a more effective manner. In response to developments a number of innovations have been progressively introduced into the dialogue on nuclear export control standards, and there have been some important achievements. In 1992 NSG participating states agreed to notify one another of cases in which they deny applications for export licences because of proliferation concerns. In 1999 the NSG began a slower and more gradual evaluation of the need to control 'intangible technology'. In 2004 the NSG adopted an end-use or 'catch-all' requirement under which an exporter would be obliged to submit any item (whether or not it is on a control list) for assessment before it is shipped to a particular, identified facility or end-user.

---

[222] Press release by the Inspector General of Police in relation to investigation on the alleged production of components for Libya's uranium enrichment programme, Kuala Lumpur, 20 Feb. 2004.

[223] According to the US official who led the discussions with Libya, Ambassador Donald Mahley, in 'Dismantling Libyan weapons: lessons learned', *Arena*, no. 10 (Nov. 2004).

One of the most important features of export controls as a non-proliferation measure is their preventive nature. However, to make them effective as such, the authorities implementing controls need accurate information about end-use and end-users during the pre-shipment phase. Enhancing the timeliness and accuracy of information and sharing it effectively among participating states is another urgent challenge for the NSG.

The Proliferation Security Initiative is one mechanism that could help to build trust and facilitate information exchange and cooperation among enforcement agencies and so enhance export control enforcement. The PSI was announced by President Bush in 2003 as a cooperative effort to facilitate seizing weapons of mass destruction and related goods in transit.[224] Although it is not specifically targeted on nuclear items, participants agreed at the July 2003 PSI meeting in Australia that Iran and North Korea are states of particular proliferation concern, and so it might be expected that shipments to these countries would be a focus of particular scrutiny by enforcement agencies.[225]

Under the PSI, states commit themselves to 'Undertake effective measures, either alone or in concert with other states', that allow them to interdict illicit transfers. Therefore, states need to introduce procedures for rapid information sharing and promise to dedicate 'appropriate resources and efforts' to such operations. The participating states also undertake to review and strengthen national legal systems to ensure that they have the necessary powers.

There is no public list of PSI participants and the states themselves have emphasized that they see the PSI as an action-oriented instrument and do not intend for it to evolve into an institution. The PSI has been described as 'a heterogeneous group' in which states participate at different levels and in different activities.[226] At least 75 states have been identified as taking part in PSI activities of one or another kind. This group includes many non-NSG states that can play an important role in combating illicit trafficking because they bestride known

---

[224] The White House, Office of the Press Secretary, 'Remarks by the President to the people of Poland', Wawel Royal Castle, Krakow, 31 May 2003, <http://www.whitehouse.gov/news/releases/2003/05/20030531-3.html>.

[225] Remarks of John R. Bolton at the Proliferation Security Initiative meeting, Paris, 4 Sep. 2003, <http://www.state.gov/t/us/rm/23801.htm>.

[226] Kulesa, L., 'Current state of the Proliferation Security Initiative and prospects for the future', Unpublished paper, SIPRI, Stockholm, July 2006.

trafficking routes, they are important centres of transit and trans-shipment, or they are countries where important fleets of commercial ships and aircraft used in international transport are registered.

Around 20 countries take part in Operational Expert Group (OEG) meetings, which are meetings of enforcement officers that can be regarded as a kind of steering committee for the PSI. These countries have the operational capabilities and expertise, inter-agency cooperation mechanisms and legal framework in place to best equip them to further the aims of the PSI.

The PSI has carried out three kinds of activity that can strengthen the capacities of enforcement authorities: interdiction operations, interdiction exercises and OEG meetings. Interdictions are not reported as an aggregate in public documents; however, according to US officials approximately two interdictions per month were carried out in 2005 and the first half of 2006.[227] Interdiction operations would be those that involve participation by two or more enforcement agencies from countries that support the PSI, rather than purely national operations. Many PSI exercises have been reported, all but one organized by OEG states.[228] Apart from their international dimension, the PSI exercises are valuable in linking different national enforcement agencies and testing cooperation arrangements between them.[229]

The OEG meetings are an opportunity for core PSI participants to work on information sharing arrangements and operational concepts for interdictions based on the experience gained in actual operations and exercises. Through these meetings an enforcement community could grow over time that develops sufficient trust to permit extensive sharing of more sensitive types of intelligence information. With the participation of Russia (after November 2004) the OEG includes many, but not all, of the most important nuclear suppliers. Ukrainian participation in the OEG has been sporadic while China, India and South Korea are probably the most important absentees.

---

[227] US Department of State, Remarks by Robert G. Joseph, Under Secretary of State for Arms Control and International Security, 'Broadening and deepening our Proliferation Security Initiative cooperation', Warsaw, 23 June 2006, <http://www.state.gov/t/us/rm/68269.htm>.

[228] For more on PSI activities and exercises see US Department of State, 'Proliferation Security Initiative logs varied activities in two years', May 2005, <http://usinfo.state.gov/is/Archive/2005/may/o3-764392.html>.

[229] E.g. the PSI exercise carried out at Frankfurt Airport in Germany in Mar. 2004 engaged the export licensing authority; the federal criminal customs service; the regional customs authority; and the federal, regional, border and airport police.

The USA has made persistent efforts to engage India in cooperation with PSI activities. China and South Korea have been deterred from participation by the public statements of North Korea, which has made it clear that it interprets PSI participation as a hostile act. Therefore, there is a concern in these countries that PSI participation could further complicate the Six-Party Talks, which are intended to engage North Korea in a dialogue with the aim of finding a solution to the nuclear crisis on the Korean peninsula.[230]

However, despite the non-participation of certain states, the development of information sharing and arrangements for practical cooperation through the PSI has the potential to make a very important contribution to the effective enforcement of export controls.

---

[230] The 6 parties are China, Japan, North Korea, South Korea, Russia and the USA. There have been 6 rounds of talks since 2003. For more on the Six-Party Talks and North Korea's nuclear programme see Kile, S. N., 'Nuclear arms control and non-proliferation', *SIPRI Yearbook 2007* (note 25), pp. 478–80.

5. Conclusions

I. Introduction

This Research Report explores the principles that underpin nuclear export controls and why they have gradually become generally recognized as important and necessary aspects of stability and security across the international community. National export controls should be seen as an important part of an integrated and mutually reinforcing system that can reduce the risk of nuclear weapon proliferation. It is accepted that transparency in nuclear-related export controls should be promoted within the framework of dialogue and cooperation among interested states.

The value of nuclear export controls has been recognized at a time of great concern over nuclear weapon proliferation because they are an instrument that can help prevent the acquisition of nuclear weapons by countries that do not already possess them. Export controls can help create an environment where international trade and cooperation in nuclear items and nuclear dual-use items can take place more safely from a non-proliferation perspective. Furthermore, export controls are likely to attract increasing attention because many observers and analysts anticipate a significant growth in civilian nuclear power worldwide over the coming decades. The need for peaceful and legitimate trade to take place with minimum risk that this trade could contribute to the development, production and use of nuclear weapons will become progressively greater.

Through their cooperation in the NSG, participating states have played an important part in generating agreement about the need for export controls. The progressive expansion of participation in the NSG has increased the number of countries with modern and comprehensive export control legislation in force. Moreover, by agreeing on a number of common elements that effective legislation needs to contain within the NSG, the main nuclear suppliers have contributed to what can be seen as an emerging international standard for an export control system. It is broadly accepted that exporters should be subject to control using a system that is clear and transparent to them and where they can be confident that rules will be applied in a consistent manner. There is widespread agreement that the control system has three critical elements: its legal form, the items that are subject to control and the principles that guide the decisions to authorize or deny any particular transaction.

First, in regard to the legal form of controls there is now wide acceptance that the export control system should be based on law, including primary legislation as well as decrees, regulations and other normative acts. More and more countries have introduced or are introducing national export control laws. This reflects both the view that laws are the best way to ensure that the rules adopted are transparent to exporters and the wider public and the fact that the process of law-making is an effective way to ensure that any established rules balance different political, economic and security interests in a fair and efficient manner. This approach helps to build the broadest base of support for the agreed rules, which increases the chances of effective implementation.

Second, the control lists developed through NSG cooperation have played a critical role in establishing international agreement on which items should be subject to controls. There are several clear examples that can be cited to illustrate this point. As discussed in chapter 4, the UN Security Council's decisions to introduce measures restricting trade in certain items with Iran and North Korea were based in part on the NSG control lists. The NSG lists also form part of EU Council Regulation 1334/2000 on export control of dual-use items. In this way the political agreement among NSG participating states to ensure that items on the NSG lists are controlled prior to export has been transformed directly into a legal obligation that is binding on all UN member states in the case of Iran and North Korea. For the 27 EU member states, a group that includes a number of important nuclear suppliers, the NSG lists now form part of the primary legislation governing exports to all countries. Furthermore, the EU dual-use export control legislation has become a model adopted by a number of other countries, including several that do not participate in the NSG. The EU has begun to expand its programme of export control outreach and assistance significantly, and in this way the NSG control lists are likely to be translated into the national laws of an even larger number of countries in the future. It is also interesting to note that the NSG control lists provided an important point of reference for countries that have recently introduced new national export control legislation, such as India and Pakistan.

The system of using lists to define the scope of export controls has been supplemented in recent years by the use of so-called catch-all controls that require authorization for certain transactions even when the items involved are not listed on the NSG trigger list. Recent experience has underlined that a system based only on control lists is difficult to reconcile with developments in industry and with the actual pattern of proliferation. To meet the requirement that export controls should not become a serious barrier to legitimate trade there is pressure to delist items that are in very widespread circulation globally. However, recent experience has underlined that such items, which may be older and produced in many countries or which might have technical specifications just below those of listed items, may contribute to nuclear weapon programmes. This was one lesson drawn from the IAEA inspections in Iraq, for example. Recognizing that inclusion on the control lists of all the items that could contribute to a programme of concern is unrealistic, in 2004 the participating states agreed to include a 'catch-all' control as part of the NSG Guidelines. Through the NSG outreach programme to non-participating states and to international organizations this decision may help to establish the principle that catch-all controls should be an element in all national export controls.

The third area where NSG cooperation has had an important effect on international nuclear export control has been the development of specific and, for the most part, objective guidelines for nuclear supply. Guidelines such as the requirement for assurances from the importing government related to non-diversion of controlled items to unsafeguarded nuclear fuel cycle or nuclear explosive activities, and the requirement for controlled items to be subject to physical protection measures that meet the highest international standards, also emphasize the point that export controls and safeguards should be seen as two interrelated elements of an integrated nuclear control system.

The guidelines are also important because they underline that if controlled items are transferred outside the jurisdiction of one country then it is important that the national authorities of the recipient should apply the same criteria as the original exporter prior to any re-export. This is the only way to maintain the integrity of the export controls applied by the original supplier. To implement this requirement it is necessary to have appropriate legislation and licensing procedures in place in the recipient country. In accord with this guideline a growing number of nuclear importers are accepting that they also need effective national export controls if they are to participate in international nuclear cooperation even though they do not themselves develop or produce controlled items.

II. Strengthening export controls

The previous section concluded that certain necessary elements of modern and effective export control legislation have been agreed on a widespread if not fully global basis. However, the specific way in which these agreed elements are reflected in national law is different in different countries. The same can be said for the administrative system needed to license exports in order to implement the laws. Although there are many and diverse approaches to organizing export licensing, there is emerging agreement on the tasks that need to be performed if licensing is to be efficient and effective. The same conclusion cannot really be reached in regard to the enforcement of export controls. The international discussion of how to enforce export controls is currently at a very early stage and advancing this dialogue should become a high priority for the NSG in the near future.

Facilitating effective national export licensing

To ensure effective export licensing, national authorities need to be able to classify or identify the items that require authorization prior to export, and they need to be able to collect and analyse information about the end-user of the controlled items and the stated end-use.

Product identificaton and classification require a technical evaluation of the specifications of the item for which export authorization is requested. The NSG technical experts have developed control lists that include elaborated definitions and detailed specifications that trigger the need for control. The lists play a key role in helping authorities determine if an item needs a licence.

In evaluating end-users, licensing authorities need detailed and current information to help determine whether the end-user is located in a country of potential concern, what products and services the end-user provides and whether there is any record of engagement in activities of concern as well as the ownership structure of the end-user. As regards end-use, the licensing authority must determine if the items can be used for the stated end-use, whether or not to require some form of end-use assurance from the importing country and whether the transfer is reasonable given the overall business plan of the end-user. This information is needed to evaluate the risk of diversion to a weapon programme.

Cooperation within the NSG plays an important role in helping national licensing authorities get access to the information they need to do their work effectively. The information that is shared about countries and programmes of concern as well as the information about licence applications that have been denied are tools that are of direct relevance to licensing officers. Moreover, the network of national licensing officers that the NSG has helped to create through sustained cooperation is itself a valuable resource that can be used to help answer specific questions during the evaluation of a licence application. The NSG has strengthened its capacity to share information, including by developing a secure electronic system that allows data to be exchanged in real time.

Enforcing nuclear export controls

The above sections present the conclusion that the NSG has made a significant contribution to strengthening export control. However, on the basis of chapters 2–4 it can also be concluded that there are still many challenges to overcome. Clandestine nuclear trafficking is now known to have contributed significantly to illegal weapon programmes in at least three countries—Iraq, Libya and North Korea. Several other countries (including Iran and Pakistan) have also drawn on illicit trafficking networks to acquire items for their nuclear programmes. In a number of these cases it is now known that items were acquired from countries that participate in the Nuclear Suppliers Group.

The checking and assessment that forms part of the licensing process can be considered one form of enforcement. However, the evidence of significant export control failures leads to the conclusion that licensing needs to be supplemented by other measures.

The screening of information presented by exporters to customs authorities could become an important element of export control enforcement through initiatives intended to strengthen security in the supply chain, such as the 2005 Framework of Standards to Secure and

Facilitate Global Trade (SAFE) being developed in the World Customs Organization and adopted by its members.[231] These initiatives require exporters to submit information to customs authorities before goods arrive at the border prior to leaving the jurisdiction of the export control authorities. The Framework of Standards also requires that this information must be in electronic form. This allows specialists to examine the electronic data and compare it with risk indicators in an effort to uncover the unlicensed export of controlled items.

Developing closer cooperation with exporters is an aspect of preventive enforcement that is beginning to attract increased attention from export control authorities. However, working more closely with industry is another area where the NSG could strengthen its efforts. The task of outreach to industry is mainly the responsibility of national export control authorities. However, the NSG should engage more strongly in discussing and reporting on national outreach programmes. As an example, the EU internal review of how member states implement dual-use export controls revealed significant differences in national approaches to export control outreach to industry. The NSG could usefully discuss the elements of national outreach programmes as well as the methodologies, materials and events that have proved to be effective in this area with a view to improving the quality of outreach efforts.

Since 1997 the NSG has organized two international seminars on the role of export controls in nuclear non-proliferation. Although representatives from industry were invited to participate on both occasions, these seminars did not address the role of industry in export control enforcement or collect the views of exporters about export control on a systematic basis. There is a strong case for seminars to interact with nuclear industry associations such as the European Atomic Forum (FORATOM).[232] In particular, dialogue with industry will be vital in attempting to modernize export controls to cope with developments such as the transfer of technology using intangible means and the increasingly international ownership structure of the global nuclear industry.

---

[231] World Customs Organization (WCO), *Framework of Standards to Secure and Facilitate Global Trade* (WCO: Brussels, 2005), <http://wcoomd.org/ie/EN/en.html>.

[232] FORATOM includes 16 national nuclear associations and almost 800 firms engaged in the nuclear industry among its members. See <http://www.foratom.org>.

Investigating, prosecuting and punishing violations of relevant laws represent another important element of export control enforcement. Some nuclear traffickers have been convicted of various export-related offences in the recent past.[233] Following the release of information about the activities of the illicit trafficking network managed by A. Q. Khan a significant number of police investigations have been initiated in different countries around the world.

It is the responsibility of states to task law enforcement authorities with responsibility for investigation and prosecution and to provide adequate resources and training for enforcement officers. However, there could be a role for the NSG in facilitating effective investigations and prosecutions. States must ensure that the frameworks for cooperation between relevant agencies outside the country are in place so that they can be available when needed to gather information and evidence. States must also establish effective penalties (which may include criminal sanctions, civil fines, publicity and restriction or denial of export privileges) sufficient to deter violations of export controls. The question of what kind of penalties provide an effective deterrent as well as an appropriate punishment for different offences should also be discussed internationally.

Closer cooperation with the IAEA to facilitate transparency

Export controls should be seen as one element in an integrated nuclear control system. Another critical element of that integrated system is a national system of accounting and control (including physical protection of nuclear material) that is tied to standards established under nuclear safeguards. The question of how to promote effective and practical synergies between the NSG, as an important body promoting export control cooperation, and international nuclear safeguards is an important one.

Exploiting the synergies between export controls and safeguards has been considered difficult because the particular approaches to information management taken by the IAEA and the NSG prevent these bodies from sharing data. A more creative approach is needed to allow

---

[233] E.g. in Dec. 2005 Henk Slebos and 2 of his companies were convicted on 5 counts of violating Dutch export law. See 'Disclosure of illicit supply networks expose weaknesses in European export control systems', *International Export Control Observer*, no. 3 (Dec. 2005/ Jan. 2006), <http://cns.miis.edu/pubs/observer/index.htmp>, p. 14–18.

the needs of the NSG and the IAEA to be met without changing existing procedures.[234] The NSG states are free to share their own information on export licences. There would be no barrier to a collective decision by the NSG that each participating state will, on an individual basis and under its own responsibility, share information with the IAEA about applications to export controlled items that have been denied for reasons related to the NSG Guidelines. Once in possession of that information, the IAEA might approach the country in which specific denied parties are located and underline to them that they have a self-interest in greater transparency in regard to the particular end-user and end-use that is causing concern among nuclear suppliers. Information released by the denied party or released under the responsibility of the state where the denied party is located could play an important role in reassuring nuclear suppliers, thereby acting as a trade-facilitating measure.

In each of these cases both the NSG and the IAEA would respect their obligations related to information protection but could act as a catalyst for decisions by states to decide freely to publish or share information related to their own nuclear exports or imports.

Strengthening nuclear export control guidelines

This Research Report describes a number of proposals currently being discussed within the NSG that are intended to strengthen nuclear export control guidelines. The adoption of the condition that an importing state should have agreed and implemented an Additional Protocol to its safeguards agreement with the IAEA as a condition for receiving trigger list items would be a logical and useful development. However, to ensure that this condition of supply does not disrupt legitimate international trade, more effort is needed to increase the number of states that have an Additional Protocol in force. At a min-

---

[234] John Carlson of the Australian Safeguards and Non-proliferation Office has pointed out that state declarations made in the framework of the 1993 Chemical Weapons Convention (CWC) are generally available to CWC states parties and can therefore be cross-checked against other available information. Carlson, J., 'Safeguards in a broader policy perspective: verifying treaty compliance', Paper presented to the Institute of Nuclear Materials Management and the European Safeguards R&D Association workshop, Changing the Safeguards Culture, Santa Fe, N.Mex., 30 Oct.–2 Nov. 2005, <http://www.asno.dfat.gov.au/index_pubs. html>, p. 4.

imum, NSG states should take the lead in ensuring that all members of the NSG have an Additional Protocol in place.

Establishing special rules to govern licensing of the most proliferation-sensitive technologies (those associated with uranium enrichment and the reprocessing of spent nuclear fuel) is also under discussion within the NSG. However, it may not be possible to reach agreement about further restrictions on the supply of sensitive technologies while the future role of nuclear power in the energy strategies of many states is undecided. A number of NSG participating states may wish to offer higher value added services in the nuclear fuel cycle if a large international market for such services develops in the future. These states may be unwilling to take steps now that could prejudice the option to enter civilian markets later. Energy policy has moved close to the top of the political agenda in many countries and regions. The development of effective nuclear non-proliferation policies requires that the process of planning the role of nuclear power in future energy strategies is completed in the shortest possible time.

One important issue that should form part of the wider discussion of nuclear non-proliferation is the future role of multinational ownership and management of nuclear facilities, in particular the most sensitive facilities, in relation to the conditions for nuclear supply. In 2004 the independent Expert Group on Multilateral Approaches to the Nuclear Fuel Cycle, commissioned by the Director General of the IAEA, completed its work, which was published in early 2005.[235] The subsequent discussion of the options laid out by the expert group among IAEA member states has been rather slow.

Recent discussions under the umbrella of the IAEA have suggested that a comprehensive multilateral system could be achieved but only in the medium to long term. However, this discussion took place at a special event organized by the IAEA Director General on the sidelines of the IAEA General Conference to examine a New Framework for the Utilization of Nuclear Energy in the 21st Century.[236] The meeting could not (and was not intended to) adopt decisions that would be binding on states.

[235] IAEA (note 185). See also Fedchenko, V., 'Multilateral control of the nuclear fuel cycle', *SIPRI Yearbook 2006* (note 59), pp. 695–98.

[236] IAEA, New framework for the utilization of nuclear energy in the 21st century: assurances of supply and non-proliferation, 50th IAEA General Conference Special Event, Vienna, 19–21 Sep. 2006, <http://www-pub.iaea.org/MTCD/Meetings/Announcements.asp?ConfID=147>. See in particular the Report of the Chairman, Charles Curtis.

It can be concluded that the adoption of conditions of supply linked to multilateral ownership and control is also likely to lie some way in the future.

III. Country-specific nuclear export controls

The NSG Guidelines are applied to all nuclear transfers and the group has not developed country-specific controls. However, as discussed in this Research Report, the NSG has recently made public statements about nuclear programmes and activities of concern in specific countries. This could be interpreted as a signal that country-specific controls might be a next step for the NSG.

After North Korea carried out a nuclear weapon test in 2006 the UN Security Council unanimously adopted Resolution 1718.[237] This resolution included provisions to prevent the transfer of nuclear technology (as well as certain other things) to North Korea. The resolution also authorized the inspection of cargo to ensure compliance with the measures adopted. The Security Council decided that all UN member states 'shall prevent the direct or indirect supply, sale or transfer to the DPRK, through their territories or by their nationals, or using their flag vessels or aircraft, and whether or not originating in their territories' of items specified in several lists that form part of the resolution. One of these lists is UN document S/2006/814, which is a list of nuclear material, equipment and technology as well as nuclear-related dual-use equipment, materials, software and related technology.[238]

It is clear that the list is closely modelled on the control lists developed by the NSG. This development, along with the adoption of similar measures related to Iran's nuclear programme, should logically require the NSG to develop specific arrangements to help implement and enforce the relevant resolutions. It is of primary importance that NSG participating states are themselves able to implement UN decisions effectively. However, given the growing focus on export control outreach in recent years, the NSG could also consider what

---

[237] UN Security Council Resolution 1718, 14 Oct. 2006.

[238] Other lists attached to the resolution are S/2006/815: Missile technology, equipment, and software; and S/2006/853: Chemical weapons precursors, dual-use chemical manu-facturing facilities and equipment and related technology, dual-use biological equipment and related technology, biological agents, plant pathogens, and animal pathogens.

can be done to help non-participating states to meet their obligations to the United Nations when the Security Council adopts country-specific measures.

IV. A global framework regulating nuclear supply

Since the early 1990s the UN Security Council has progressively taken closer and closer interest in preventing nuclear proliferation, which was identified as a threat to international peace and security in a joint statement by the heads of state and government of the countries serving on the Security Council in 1992. However, this joint statement has not been translated into a legal form that could create a global nuclear non-proliferation framework. Therefore, it is still the NPT that provides the closest approximation of a global legal framework for non-proliferation.

While the NPT has near-universal participation, a growing number of questions are being asked about whether it can continue to provide a global framework for non-proliferation efforts. It has not been possible to adapt the NPT, although the conditions in the global nuclear industry have changed fundamentally since the 1960s, when the treaty was negotiated. Geopolitical and strategic conditions have also changed fundamentally since the 1960s in ways that have a direct bearing on issues that are central to the objectives of the treaty. In particular, the role that nuclear weapons played in the strategies of the recognized nuclear weapon states has changed since the end of the cold war.

The changed conditions, in the nuclear industry in particular, create challenges for export control. The number of nuclear suppliers has increased and the places where those suppliers are to be found are no longer concentrated in the countries that have been traditional partners in export control cooperation. Moreover, many analysts anticipate that the number of countries able to supply nuclear or nuclear-related dual-use items will continue to grow. The number of countries operating significant nuclear facilities is also expected to grow, as are the number of facilities being operated in countries that already have a nuclear infrastructure in place. This will multiply the number of nuclear end-users and the scale of international nuclear trade (including services that facilitate trade such as freight forwarders and companies that specialize in helping exporters prepare and submit export documents).

The way in which industry does business is changing as well. The nuclear industry is no longer 'stovepiped' within countries, and a business model based on international cooperation is becoming more common. Research and development is already being carried out by multinational companies on a global scale, involving laboratories and facilities in different countries. These cooperation partners are also likely to exchange personnel through visits and attachments and they are likely to be linked through electronic communications networks that facilitate intangible transfers of technology. The number and speed of electronic transactions and communications are already challenging traditional approaches to export control.

To meet these challenges a global framework that creates common and agreed standards for control is one logical development. As noted above, it is highly unlikely that these standards could be developed within the NPT. However, by linking activities carried out in its different constituent parts, the UN might provide a global framework for developing and approving the necessary standards.

Export controls within a UN framework

Recent proposals that are described in this Research Report could form the basis on which a global export control framework might develop, by linking actions taken in different parts of the UN in a coherent manner.

The proposal for a nuclear supply treaty was put forward by the IAEA Director General. Such a treaty could establish the rights and obligations of states in regard to the access to peaceful nuclear power in a more precise manner than is currently the case in the NPT. It would in effect specify with greater clarity one of the pillars of the NPT and would support, rather than compete with or replace, the existing law.

A common and cooperative effort to implement UN Security Council Resolution 1540 could be the basis for the adoption of global export control standards by identifying successful elements of modern and comprehensive export control legislation and spreading best practices in licensing and enforcement.

Concern about politically motivated attempts to deny access to the fuel needed for reactors at nuclear power plants could be a motive for states to develop national uranium enrichment capabilities that also give rise to proliferation concerns. The establishment of an international mechanism for assured supply of nuclear power-reactor fuel could reduce the likelihood that states will initiate national uranium enrichment programmes. The same logic applies to facilities intended to recycle used fuel.

The states participating in the NSG would have an important role to play in all of these interlinked activities. Moreover, the group itself would be a convenient location in which to discuss whether and how such an approach might be developed. The NSG has convened working groups in the past to act as a focal point for the discussion of particular issues related to nuclear export control. This mechanism might be an appropriate forum for relevant officials from the NSG participating states to informally discuss the merits of working for a global framework for modern and effective export control, and the ways and means by which such a process could be advanced.

Index

The manufacturer's authorised representative in the EU for product safety is
Oxford University Press España S.A. of el Parque Empresarial San Fernando de
Henares, Avenida de Castilla, 2 – 28830 Madrid (www.oup.es/en or product.
safety@oup.com). OUP España S.A. also acts as importer into Spain of products
made by the manufacturer.